LYRIC POSTMODERNISMS

Lyric Postmodernisms

An Anthology of Contemporary Innovative Poetries

edited by Reginald Shepherd

Counterpath Press
Denver, Colorado
2008

Counterpath Press
Denver, Colorado
www.counterpathpress.org

Printed in the United States of America

Library of Congress Cataloging-in-Publication Data

Lyric postmodernisms : an anthology of
contemporary innovative poetries / edited by Reginald Shepherd.
p.   cm.
ISBN 978-1-933996-06-6 (pbk. : alk. paper)
1. American poetry.
I. Shepherd, Reginald, 1963– II. Title.
PS613.L97 2008
811.008—dc22
2007045456

Contents

MARJORIE WELISH

ELIZABETH WILLIS

Introduction

This anthology brings together the work of twenty-three highly accomplished poets of diverse geographical, ethnic, gender, and aesthetic backgrounds whose work combines lyricism and avant-garde experimentation in a new synthesis I call, after Wittgenstein, lyrical investigations. Their work explores the poem as a form of thinking, a thinking-out and thinking-through. As Kathleen Fraser points out, "Wittgenstein's foregrounding of the term 'investigation' in his *Philosophical Investigations* sets forth a *practice* of coming to the world without certainty, but rather with curiosity, *un*belonging to an established ordering, an openness to ambiguity and the unfinished . . . even the untried." These poets discover, create, and explore new territories in the intersections between lyric enchantment and experimental interrogation. They innovate and recreate while still drawing on and incorporating the lyric past and present. Their critical art is also a celebration of the riches of the lyric tradition. The presences of classical mythology and Shakespeare in the work of many of these poets, as well as their diverse engagements with history, may be seen as one sign of their dual approach to originality as both Baudelaire's search for the new and the return to (plural) origins. Many if not most would agree with Elizabeth Willis when she writes that "I would place my work among those who recognize an evolving relation to both the 'traditional' and the 'new' and who tend to recognize *as* new this reconfiguring or re-engagement with traditions."

These poets integrate the traditional lyric's exploration of subjectivity and its discontents, the modernist grappling with questions of culture and history and language's capacity to address and encompass those questions, and the postmodernist skepticism toward grand narratives and the possibility of final answers or explanations, toward selfhood as a stable reference point, and toward language as a means by which to know the self or its world. Nathaniel Mackey notes the homophony of "lyre" and "liar," pointing out that such a wariness toward or outright distrust of language, "promoting check over enchantment," has a long if sometimes insufficiently acknowledged history.

All of these poets are deeply engaged in exploring and interrogating the relations of conception and perception, with how mind both makes its way through a world not of its own making and how mind makes a world of its own out of the world it is given: they explore both the possibilities and the limitations of this world-made-mind's world-making. As Cole Swensen asks, "Does poetry try to reflect the world in some kind of clarifying way, or does it try to construct an alternative world . . . ?" In literary critic M.H. Abrams' formulation, is the poem a mirror or is it a lamp? This is a question to which there is no permanent or universal answer, and each of these poets has his or her own response or range of responses. These poems are both products of and rejoinders to the world from which they emerge and to which they contribute, a world by which they are conditioned but not determined.

Martha Ronk writes that "My work exists in the interrogative mood, whether or not a question mark appears at the end of a line." All of these poets begin with questions. How to sustain or recover an authentic self (however that self is defined and/or constructed) and a rich and accurate expressiveness (in whatever terms one expresses expression) in a thoroughly textualized, hypermediated world of what Jean Baudrillard calls simulations, in which every experience is either simulacral or has always already been experienced before? (These concerns are obviously specific to certain social, economic, and cultural levels of the developed world's consumer societies of the spectacle. A lack of reality is not most people's biggest problem, even in America—quite the opposite, in fact.) Martine Bellen asserts that "Language represents a way of ratifying one's existence." These poets write in a context in which none of the terms of this statement—language, representation, personal existence, and the possibility of ratification or affirmation—can be taken for granted. As if in acknowledgment of this flux and uncertainty regarding the very ground of experience, Bellen goes on to write "I am not mine." These poets' work provides diverse, contingent, and often partial answers to the questions with which I began, in poems whose tactics range from the playful, the interrogative, the minimalist, the ironic, the lyrical, the extravagant, and even the sublime, sometimes coexisting, sometimes operating by turn.

Before all these questions, these poets begin with the potentially enabling or crippling question of the lyric itself. As Derrida asks, what thing is poetry? (I think these poets would reply that it is not a thing but an activity, not a noun but a verb.) What does the lyric mean in our contemporary post-everything world, one that has been described as depthless, fundamentally inauthentic, and at if not past the end of history? What does it mean to be a poet, to choose this most marginal mode of discourse in social and historical circumstances in which all discourse sometimes seems to have been emptied of meaning, content, or value? (One definition of the contemporary poet: someone who's not over it all just yet.) Kathleen Fraser writes of poetry as a response to "the pollution of speech and thought that threatens from every quarter." How one responds to that constantly metastasizing contamination, and whether it can be effectively responded to at all, haunts every poet in this volume.

Artistically as well as philosophically, we live in a time "when there is no recognized critical aesthetic," as Mei-mei Berssenbrugge points out. Ours is a decentered contemporary American literary and artistic world in which there is no agreement even on what practitioners of ostensibly the same art form are doing or trying to do, let alone on those efforts' means or aims or how they could be evaluated. Timothy Liu notes that "American poetry is a Babel," with everyone singing a dialect of one, or perhaps of his or her particular tribe. But the Babelogue that is contemporary American poetry can also be seen as a space of opportunity and possibility: we are living not just in a time of uncertainty and suspicion (of language, of selfhood, of history), but in an unusually open period of poetic exploration and discovery, very much including rediscovery.

As Brenda Hillman writes in her essay "On Song, Lyric, and Strings":

> It's hard to know what *lyric* means for post-romantics, post-symbolists, post-modernists and post-postmodernists. [RS: Not to mention post-avant-gardists and post-contemporaries.] Lyric is an element in poetry, not a type, rendering human emotion in language; attention to subjective experience in a song-like fashion seems to be key in all definitions of lyric. . . . Once lyric meant unbroken music, but since the nineteenth century, it may be broken. It cries out in singular, dialogic or in polyphonic protest. There is the question of the individual "singer," not to mention the individual lyre or the famous problem

of the solitary self. . . . Since the twentieth century unseated all certainty, the
lyric is rendered on torn, damaged or twisted strings. A lyric poet sings boldly
and bluntly to the general populace or is visited quietly and obliquely by the
distressed hero who needs an oracle.

None of the techniques of postmodernism—syntactic fracture or de-
formation, quotation, pastiche, collage, montage, cinematic jump-cuts,
polyvocality or multiplication of voices, irony, parody, the mixing of cul-
tural levels (breaking down the barriers of "high" and "low" culture) and
the mingling of kinds of diction and discourse, intentional catachresis
(incorporating the "inappropriate," inviting error), associative rather than
linear logic, seriality and juxtaposition instead of narrative or extended
meditation—is new or unique. Open any page of *The Waste Land*, of *The
Cantos*, or of *Ulysses* and you will find them. What is different is the uses
to which they are put. While most of the Anglo-American modernists,
engaged in the desire and pursuit of the whole, used these methods to try
to achieve a new and more true synthesis, many contemporary artists who
might be called postmodern employ such devices to refute the very possi-
bility of synthesis. There is no whole toward which they strive, only holes
upon which they stumble, and many find the notion of totality entirely
too totalitarian. Proceeding by means of breakage (formal, intellectual,
psychological, emotional), they simply point, helplessly, hopelessly, and
sometimes gleefully (there is a joy in smashing things, after all) to the
pieces. But as Marjorie Welish points out, "The devices that make a poem
literature can themselves be investigated, engaged, and thus refreshed."
Methods and modes do not have inherent meanings, and forms can en-
gage with many different feelings.

   Although the idea of the broken lyric (one that I borrow from poet
Cynthia Cruz) is highly suggestive and useful in thinking about the poets
assembled in this book, none of them is content to rest (however restlessly
or even restively) among fragments, to admit disjunction and be done.
Martha Ronk insists "I am not interested in single words set in white
space, but in joinery." Cole Swensen emphasizes her interest "in connec-
tions and relationships—at times more than in the things they bring to-
gether." The brokenness of discourse, of identity, of the social field, is
not the end point but the beginning, one that can be turned toward pos-
sibility rather than either despair or blank-eyed resignation. Timothy Liu
characterizes the opening toward the potentials inherent in loss as a move-

ment from song to writing, and parallels it with a Blakean journey from innocence to experience, abandoning paradise without renouncing the longing for it. Cole Swensen writes that for her, "The very point where sense begins to break down is also where it begins to open out."

Peter Gizzi describes a postmodern form of Keatsian negative capability toward which he aspires (or rather, to which he aspires to be open, allowing it to come to him, not directed by his will or his desire), a force moving through the place and time of writing that is "both a construction of self and an emptying of self—not autobiographical but autographical— flexible enough to accommodate figures, things, voices, documentation; to combine, build and dissolve being, boundaries—to somehow let the poem become itself." Most if not all of the contributors to this volume also seek to occupy that space which is no space, to be that one who is no one and everyone. As Martha Ronk puts it, "The whole seems to teeter and to fail, certainly to defy logic, but in the most satisfying moments, in the failure of absolute congruity, to create new constructs." This book collects and celebrates some of those new constructs.

In their great diversity, these highly accomplished poets all participate in a shared though varied project, yet they have rarely been thought of together. By highlighting their common goal of expanding the boundaries of what can be done in poetry, pushing forward the limits of the sayable, sometimes (in Brenda Hillman's phrase) singing against singing, this collection sheds new light on their work, including work a reader may feel that he or she already knows, by showing its interconnections. My hope is thereby to reveal a new constellation of contemporary American poetry, one formed by the continuation, expansion, and self-questioning of the Modernist project into the postmodern era, which sometimes seems hostile to the lyric and its ever-renewed and ever-renewing possibilities. None of these writers has given up a faith in the lyric, however broken or transfigured. All seek to discover and/or recover, in the words of a perhaps unlikely forebear, what can be made of a diminished thing, or even if that thing (if it really is a single thing) is actually diminished at all. Bin Ramke writes that "Poetry is what we have in lieu of explanation, and in place of consolation." But, activity and object, it is something that we have.

This book includes generous selections from each poet, so that a reader can get a sense of the writer's work as a whole. It's important to include a substantial representation of each contributor, rather than a cursory sampling, since it is often a poet's other work that teaches us how to read any given poem of hers or his. Wherever possible, I have also included uncollected work that, even if published, might be difficult to track down.

The book also includes many longer poems or excerpts from such works, which provide sustained examples of each writer's poetics and practice. The long poem, particularly the sequential or serial poem, is a significant mode in modern and contemporary American poetry, though it is also one that anthologies, in their focus on the brief and easily quotable "anthology piece," tend to neglect. Many of these poets explore different forms of the long poem, eschewing narrative or extended meditation in favor of what M. L. Rosenthal and Sally Gall have called the modern poetic sequence, an elastic and capacious mode that incorporates fragmentation and condensation, and the intensities usually associated with the brief lyric, within a larger though nonlinear structure, producing a rhizomatic art of subterranean networks and submerged connections. As Rosenthal and Gall write, "Intimate, fragmented, self-analytical, open, emotionally [and intellectually and formally] volatile, the sequence meets the needs of modern sensibility even when the poet aspires to tragic or epic scope." Sequentiality can also read as a way to highlight the necessarily failing attempt to grasp the vastness of scale and multiplicities of identities that constitute America. Some of the forerunners of such poetic sequences include Ezra Pound's *The Cantos*, William Carlos Williams's *Paterson*, Gertrude Stein's *Stanzas in Meditation*, H.D's *Trilogy*, George Oppen's *Discrete Series*, Langston Hughes's *Montage of a Dream Deferred*, Louis Zukofsky's *A*, and Charles Olson's *The Maximus Poems*. All attempt to balance scope and focus, diachrony and synchrony, structure and detail, recreating the poem minute by minute while also reaching for some larger if sometimes asymptotic goal.

I also include aesthetic statements from each contributor, from which this introduction has quoted and paraphrased extensively. These are some of the most self-conscious poets about what they are doing and why since the High Modernists, whose inheritors and continuators they are. Such statements, in which contributors discuss their work, their influences, their aims, and their poetics in general, are invaluable in situating and providing a point of entry for complex poetry that is sometimes seen as "difficult" or challenging.

By including both uncollected poems and aesthetic statements, this anthology gives the reader something that she or he cannot find elsewhere even in the unlikely event that he or she is familiar with the work of all of these poets.

While there have been many interesting and valuable anthologies of new poetry in the past several years, they have tended to be somewhat narrow either in their chronological scope or in their definitions of what constitutes innovative poetry. No anthology has brought these contemporary poets together as writers experimenting and exploring within the lyric tradition to expand that tradition's boundaries. These lyric postmodernists bring together Duncan and Berryman, Zukofsky and Bishop, Spicer and Auden, in a new poetic synthesis, one that has been very influential on newer generations of poets.

Reginald Shepherd
October 2007
Pensacola, Florida

LYRIC POSTMODERNISMS

Bruce Beasley

Toward a Poetics of Monstrosity

1.

Pound writes somewhere that poems are all "pith and gist": all core, that means to me, all crux, all inwardness. As Rilke asks in another context, "Where for this inside is there an outside?" The poem for me is a monstrous body, its surface all exposed inside, brain and lung and heart chamber and viscera, appalling and fascinating to stare into.

2.

My uncle, a physician, dislikes ambiguity, the untestable hypothesis. He used to call me up after reading my poems and bellow that I was "just an intellectual snob." "You need to write a glossary for each of your poems," he'd insist, "to EXPLAIN YOUR SYMBOLISM so people will know what the hell you're talking about, man!"

3.

"When the monster comes along," Rosamond Purcell writes, "the ground begins to slip."

4.

Italians have an expression I love: *rimanere in forse,* to "remain in perhaps," not to know, for a while. Like Keats' negative capability, it's a soothing respite from the "irritable reaching" of the intellect toward knowledge and fact. A *dispossession* of the experience. To stay in perhaps, to linger with the eroticized body of the temporarily or permanently unknown.

5.

"Look, Daddy, there's paradise," my four-year-old son Jin said to me one day. We were cleaning our way through an old junk drawer. When I finally distinguished where in the mounds of old coins and photographs and crumpled playing cards he meant me to find paradise, I saw two garish red casino cubes; pair o' dice.

6.

The conjoined bodies, the multiple personalities of each word. Homonyms coinhabiting the same flesh of letters. Each word's legions of selves struggling for primacy. *Passion* is suffering, is emotion, is rage, is zeal, is lust, is the Crucifixion. With language as its body, how can the poem not grow excrescences, overlapping limbs? Obliquity, extremity: the too-much, the not-enough, the ill-understood, the anomalous mix. *Ellipsis*, a leaving-out, means etymologically "a leaving in."

7.

The *monstrance* is the jeweled container that holds aloft the consecrated Host.

8.

Monstrous: extraordinary in a way to incite wonder; deviating greatly from the natural: malformed; having the appearance of a monster; shockingly wrong.

9.

The monster is created to give an outward form to a banished inner extremity: a dread, a rage, a *passion* that can't be made to stay inside, can't be acknowledged as our own. The *monster* (from *monore*, to warn; *monstrare*, to show) is what warns us, what shows or de*monstrates* us: a prodigy, an omen, urgently interpretable and nevertheless deeply alienating and strange.

If a poem is a place of extremity—emotional, linguistic, spiritual—no gloss is going to assimilate its monstrous body—phoneme, syllable, image, chant, word.

10.

In *The Wonderful Wizard of Oz,* a man of straw without a brain, who *thinks,* obsessively, about how much he wants the capacity to *think.* Brain-craving, Wizard-craving, though the Wizard's no wizard, and the brain he gets is anything but a brain. The twenty-year restoration of Leonardo's *Last Supper,* as if not only the painting but the sacrament it depicts—matter turned to spirit, bread to sacrificed body of Christ—could revert to some original state of wholeness. The *restoration* (spiritual, psychic, emotive, cellular) of my nephew as he undergoes another kind of violent sacramental transformation through chemotherapy and radiation to drive the leukemic cells from his blood. I mean to *estrange* the ordinary story and its language. Let its monstrous body emerge: portent, omen, monstrance-gleam. Stuck for a while at least in *perhaps.* And that's *what the hell I'm talking about.*

The Vanishing Point

> *The painting has vanished. The icon remains.*
> —Robert Payne, on Leonardo's *Last Supper*

To lessen the impact of the blanks,

a beige watercolor now covers the gaps
where Leonardo's pigment's
unsalvageable,
though for twenty years the restorers have scraped

through centuries of grime
& the refectory's
kitchen-grease,
through the retouched
retouchings, strata of varnish & glue,

as though back down
to the sacral,
the original
turquoise & lapis, the lost
fingerbowls & Judas-
spilled salt—

as though down to the last
supper itself, the first
liturgy of blood & flesh, so mingled
with betrayal
(the decayed restorations
of Judas
flaking away)

what restorer's scalpel can scrape them apart?

*

Napoleon's bored cavalry
scratched out the apostles' eyes,
& steaming dung from their horses
left white streaks of mold down the fresco.
& the monks hacked away Christ's feet
for a more commodious kitchen door,
& an American bomb
crushed the ceiling & apse
all around the sandbagged
Supper, left it
exposed to two years of rains.

& now tourists of the restoration
must walk
through a labyrinth
of glass chambers
with wind-machines & antibacterial carpet
to purify their dust
& bioeffluents
(sweat, dandruff, car exhaust, boot-dirt), to

slow
the inexorable encroachment of the blanks.

*

Christ, at the vanishing point. He's caught
exactly in the cracked
spine of the book where I try to stare down
the chipped image I remember

through scaffolding in Milan. Green
mold over His fingers
as they reach for the bread of His life.
In a half-ripped seam
where the binding's unraveling:
blue robes toward the loaf & the light,
red for Passion toward the wine & the dark, Judas

shoved back from Him as though by a blast.

*

If I have been unable to do,
Leonardo wrote in his notebook, under
"Epitaph": *if I* . . .
& there the sentence
trails away, unfinished
as whatever it was he meant his life to do . . .

*

"a surface completely ruined,
disintegrating into tiny scales of color
falling off the wall.
It's enough to make a person
want to shoot herself"
        —the restorer

Vasari, 1556: the Last Supper is already only *a muddle of blots.*

"This is not Leonardo. It is merely

fragments of bottom layers of the underlying original"
    —critic of the restoration

Lord, is it I?

                          floodwater under the painting

two feet high

    La pittura é rovinata tutta

"The question is whether to attempt to recover an original
that is at best in a fragmentary state"

If I have been
unable to do, if I . . .

Drink ye, all of it, for this is my blood

*

Zachary, at the vanishing point. T-
lineage acute lymphoblastic
leukemia. At seven,
Pokémon in his hand,
his face *a muddle of blots*, sourceless
bruises. Feed-
tube through his nose. Ativan
hallucinations. Prednisone
tablets tucked into Jell-O.

Methadone-
wean,
after two months on morphine.
*The chemo's
got to get in there & blast
all those mean cells away. It's
supposed to make you sick, that means
you're mowing down all the bad guys inside you*

Verily
the traitor's hand
dips with me, into this dish . . .

*

The underlying
original inside
me, sfumato,
in its smoke-haze of squamous flakes:
if I leach
down to it, with solvents
under microscopes, scalpel-scrub
of disintegrated grime & lacquer, down
to the gesso's
fundament, to
the "grotesquely feminine"
lips of Christ? What's left
if the accretions,
layer by layer, fall away, & the glazed
opacity of the first pigment,
fungus-overgrown, betrayal-mingled, crumbles off the wall?

*

—Dream-stare
into the alabaster masks, no
eye-holes, of the Customs guards,
on the border
of Georgia,
on Zachary's hospital grounds:
& the guard
whose hair is blowing
away, in clumps,
confiding
It's supposed to feel
miserable, like this.
That's how you can tell
it's made

good . . .

*

Among the possible
modes of failure,

post-remission:
mediastinal mass, recurrence
of blast-cells in the marrow—

Then the requisite
irradiation of the brain
& spinal column where the leukemia's
occulted—

("a more toxic approach
may increase the likelihood of a cure")

Sacrament
demanding blood, & flesh—

*

Re-
touch, Christ, that dipped

sop, that knife-blade in Peter's fist. Pass
over (lamb's
blood on every door)

& over the molting
color-scales. Pass
over Zachary, in his sleep:
bruise by bruise
wipe clean.

*The picture
is utterly ruined*

That thou doest, do quickly:

Scour, acid-
burn, down
to the point

of the disease's
vanishing

*

  lying
original
   smoke-haze:
if I leach
     solvent

  disintegrated

fundament
  "grotesquely feminine"
            left
opacity   first
        betrayal

—Dream-stare

*

When the workmen's
pick-axes loosened whole crusts

of paint, the monks
nailed them back on, so Doubting

Thomas' finger points
now to that hammer-healed

paint-wound
The irrecoverable whole

—A line
of poetry is a chance,

said Hugo Ball,
to get rid of all the filth

that clings to language
—& that crumbles

everything in the cleaning
so that the *point,*

whatever it once
was, vanishes,

like the rice-grains
of Leonardo's lapis, under

microscope, scraped
down & reaffixed

so you can barely tell
what grime's

expunged along the fracture-
lines, what

incrustations
of overlaid varnish & inbred

soot must be suffered
to remain

*

At the point
of origin, also the vanishing:

through www.newprayer.com
a radio transmitter
will set loose your supplication
at the site of the Big Bang
("why not send our prayers directly
to the last known
location of God?")

& hound
down the gone
One

(prepaid account for 20 prayers, $75)

—The diagrammed
perspective lines
toward the vanishing point
at Christ's head: like an assassin's
rifle-sight

Signal-scatter, into the cosmic
background radiation

To transmit
your prayer
to the Big Bang now, click here

*

In the paint's
caesura, the beige
gaps, where any
conclusion whatsoever

may be drawn

what Christ-face
undiscovered underneath
stares & crumbles, waits
still for the traitor's lifted hand?

waits
for the oncologist's lifted hand—

*

Mow down,
Christ, the bad

inside:
amateur-flaws in the overpainting, restoration-
   lies
originations obscured in
   smoke-haze
  if I leech

off You,   solve, salve
me

   Reintegrate from the
fundament   De
profundis

*

Should the Supper
(sandbagged, or scaffolded, or trapped
at the glass labyrinth's

core)
be forced to *last*?

Or allowed
its vanishing,
its last-known
location
somewhere among the irradiated

blanks? Set
loose my supplication,
while Zachary's blast cell
count is down
to nothing,

to hammer-healed

Christ,
at the vanishing point, the click,
O-
mega,
the last
Unknowable (restored
to disintegration),

irrecoverable
original,

the last-known . . .

The Scarecrow's Supplication

> *So the Wizard unfastened the Scarecrow's head . . . and mixed a cup of cereal*
> *with pins and needles. Then he filled the top of the Scarecrow's head with the*
> *mixture . . . The Scarecrow decided to think. He thought so hard that the pins*
> *and needles began to stick out of his brains.*
>
> —L. Frank Baum, *The Wonderful Wizard of Oz*

Tinman   hatchet-arm's   rustblotch
Monkeywings   dullgold brick's click & hiss

hiss of witchmelt   Poppydose, & doze
& everything emeralded, skywritten surrender

er   Broomstick in the grip. Crushed
rubyslippers under the ripped-up

stormcellar's cement rootstock   she said
aunt'sface in the cornstalks, in the seeall

witches' glass   Crow on crow on crow on crow
unscared in a field It watched over

I It   alphabethalves   Secondhalf only
O through Z   Oz   Havenot   Stuff

ing through rainworn seams   Backstuck pole
Untraversable   desertspread between Kansas

& SouthWitch what
slipper's heelclick

what luffed balloontether
& green ribs of Ozthrone

what housewhirl
or match struck

to straw or lionclaw
or hammerheads' smack & flatten

what goldstep's thousand days
skull-gives

& headwithin
go thinkings straw-to-straw-to-straw

to needlepin eyesbehind not a neuron   not a synapse   not a white
matter not a convolution not an

an   not an *a* through an *n*
Oz's   needlestore, & straw's needles   Roost-crows on straw

To be afraid   to speak Dorothy's
To speak Dorothy's unwitchwords   Come

Come back   *w*
itch

izard in
aw

bra
str

Brainstraw   Take back
these needles, Ozlord   O-through-Z   need dulls

headstuff & stab
if that's all the brain you can give

Martine Bellen

Time Travel and Poetry

The following interview will take place in the middle of the night.
Punctuated by shakuhachi music, and wind.

Lady Murasaki: Watching water birds on the lake increase in number.
Taking note of flowers. The way clouds travel season to season. The
moon. Frost. Why would you purport to know the body of my land?
Carnal. "To know" in the most intimate sense. Through the senses.

Martine Bellen: Language represents a way of ratifying one's existence.

That the lover must absent himself for yearning, desire, to occur. That
writing embodies absence. "Shunyata. Form is exactly shunyata, shunyata
exactly form."
Poetry probes what is heard when peering behind painted screens.
That which is not known. Carnal. That which is closest to us.
Lady Murasaki, you are not known by your own name but by one derived
of your father's title.

I am not mine.

When the Emperor makes an error
the world is set in turmoil.

When the poet sets pen to paper

Sets off on a journey

Begins to right it.

In the Heian period, writing in the Japanese language was private.
Men lost control of their language, women their bodies.

                                                 Once a woman
is known she becomes a character in a romance that waits to be opened.
Carnal. She becomes poetry. We desire to know her and yet . . .

                                        Words on a page or tracks across
snow from a strange bird, indelible writing, melting writing. Strange
white bird that travels from snow to cloud. Poetry.

During Japan's feudal period (1573–1868), Inoue Mitsuo (author of *Space in Japanese Architecture*) writes, Japanese architecture allowed for the movement of space. Rooms of a home were scattered randomly, not organized geometrically. Space was discreetly revealed, revealed discreetly. Shunyata.

He compares movement-oriented Japanese architecture to episodic literature such as *The Tale of Genji*.

What might happen when a girl walks out a door and begins talking. A home with rooms scattered randomly.

The way lines of poetry slip past one another. Rooms connected by elongated "U"s or zigzagging corridors and natural sounds linger in negative space—rooms we open in to. Rooms that speak a foreign language. Rooms that write a different language than they speak.

Hayao Miyazaki's film *Howl's Moving Castle* sets Japanese aesthetics against a westernized landscape. A slippage in direction, meaning, syntax. The way a line might wander off and speak to a stranger. A spell might be cast. Powerful words that change the course of a life. Words originating from an older/other time. Older/other place. Order. Words that have traveled far and long to meet you.

Terrifying Creatures

We met like bits of drifting duckweed

It is dawn and a woman lies in bed
with another woman's lover. His costume,
such glossy beaten silk that one cannot tell
if he is parting or a part of mist
and memory, the path is endless

a cliff with water rushing down its face

———————

if a bird flutters near flowers

if it flies into the candle's flame small as a bean

if it burns. if it burns.

Sitting on your floor playing with dolls. Manipulating
their arms, mouths, mating

If a bird cries for its mate it can be consoled by placing a mirror before it.
If a mother's blood is smeared on ancient coins, the currency will find her
children no matter how long it circulates. The biological system of love.
We love to see the new straw moon spread across an absent sky. night
with a clear moon, a glass of clear water. we hurried to rise with the dew.

Terrifying creatures with
spindly arms and legs live on
a sliding screen in a stormy sea.
I open that screen, look into the eyes
of a man who travels alone.

———————

On the first day of the first month meanings become clear:

We dream my parents have sent a boat to fetch us. A messenger arrives at the house where we were born. When the guest feels he has seen every-thing, he takes a sudden turn or opens a door, and before him is a fence of plum trees and a wall with wandering vines. Troublesome ghosts and unhealthy objects such as ships arrive regularly forcing their way into your most private place and scattering your furnishings; in between it looks to be a mountain, only there is no mountain. nor any guest. Although this moment is spectacular we wouldn't want it to last a thousand years.

———————————

Our parting-fires, wild pinks. You apologize for having to go and for so long, halfway through our journey. Though one makes one's face look squished as if about to cry, it is no use, no tears will come.

                                  The noise of mosquitoes in my ear is thunderous, and I eat silver noodles to bring me luck, to lead me to you.

Dear old lover,

The reverse, which is a window, has shut. You are no longer behind every-thing. Soon there will not be any more pain because of you

How I imagine death

Letting go and slipping past. Shipping away.

from *Tales of Murasaki*

DREAM OF THE SPIDER BRIDGE

I

Because she found darkness in the recesses of home most frightening

Because clouds traced sad lines across the sky

she put out
to sea

  So careful to choose lucky days for our beginnings

The honeyed-moon, two nights past full

One envies waves that must return whence they came but rows them to
avoid tangles

even the skies have closed down

"even the mind has gone
against invertebrate habits"

The boat hiding inside a depression, a brushed tear induced by the splash-
ing of our oars and calls of overhead geese, wild and barely visible, not
storied to be otherwise

"I caught the ferry
where I never caught it before"

Mother was with me holding hand to heart but so severely I thought of
alligators known to eat their young and other cold things. The sky was
darkening and I asked him if perhaps this was an omen and we should
set out in another way but spoke so quietly because he seemed particu-
larly rough and as changing as the sky that threatened rain. Many fears
ran through the whole of me; I wanted him to stop, tensed my limbs my
voice left first,

"It was dawn inside
when I made ready to leave"

II

Too long a winter's day to make way through these snows where uncom-
monly elegant fishers dwell and rustics who could not identify the music
were lured out into sea-winds there to catch their death

"I will take to you
a bottle of Soju and fried fish"

An old woman whose only remaining task was to die brought to the tem-
ple as an offering for a better position a Chinese coxcomb box. A man

who did not recognize her came into her dream. No visit at all would have exceeded the one in which an enormous passage of time was created and in it two players took and untook the same stones for all eternity without affecting the larger disposition of forces. It can be set up as a game and the desired results can be known and yet at the point when the situation looks as it was foretold all other directions appear altered and even now the result is at a distance. These never-tended gardens covering foxes and owls howling in unpruned groves morning into night.

She had been closer than she ever deserved or knew

III

we should not allow it such a hold on us

IV

Her hair collected as it fell

bamboo

ten feet long stuffed in incense jars and test tubes

sowed herbs

what is left, after, or the worn path inside

wormwood

"And I had thought then that I was unhappy; it is no better now"

Fifth day of the fifth month (the most propitious)

Mother said in the big book all is written and so I began my own small one with myself as a peripheral character to trick I wrote it on azure rice paper and with my left hand. I chose words by others rather than my own. Mother, I ask, are you referring to predestination? Is there nothing I can do with only the day of death important enough to be marked? So many numbers writes god the mathematician, keeper of deeds and destruction. Abacus and rosary. She binds my fingers and toes in tape and bleeds me. I am your mother and must prepare for it, my duty to keep you small and in order.

v

peepers and glass frogs. It was a moment of recognition, when the scene changes and we realize reversals. That is what makes for tragedy. Flip-flop of the magnetic field. It can be tracked. If A = B then who am I?

I love to watch you
  the way you position your workman hands
    and dig through my nipples
      the color, for example, is dried red
        my star looks grape a finch dressed in raspberry sauce

the day you position your hips

your back becomes the walking night away nothing becomes you better

The falconer offered a sampling of his take. Everything he brings together in himself for me to receive but he cannot dream truth and it is that which ties with ribbons this world to the other. A Judas tree grows on the moon. It sheds shadows and he calls me traitor. Letters filled with warm vowels; I return avowals. He knows better than most what a mistake it is to get attached to a place or trust a life that is not ours to trust. I write by firefly. It is the mating call, the need for more. I never came away without some small thing that seemed precious, touching things, annoying things.

She seemed in danger of falling in love

In her garden, however, was not the smallest suggestion of disorder:

Yellow yamabuki reflected
in the pond as if about to join
its own image. Moon passed moss
carpet. Abeyance beneath

a star-filled bowl, jewels worn
by the Pleiades

Bringer of Light

VI

They looked for her where they thought she might be.

I made no move myself to try the river for the black cloud boiled overhead
and sonorous strains of royal deer scattered about the forest where red
silks were beaten to a soft luster and gossamer of delicate saffron stirred in
waters once expected to find a muddy mood floating upon it one found
a bright yellow. Also, dew collected on her evening face she had so briefly
to find a passage over a thousand years.

Beauty and pain had come to appear much alike.

TALE OF THE ANCIENT PRINCESS

I

Moaning of prayers in morning air.

The world cast inside, a cicada-cage made of bamboo.

In search of a nunciary—overtones echo home.

Cloud echoes cloud,
        clouds break like bread and steam rises
                into the stream that flows through a Stupa.

She no longer welcomed
familiar spirits who left messages
in layers of dust and in motes, their bon mots

Wild grasses strangled the tamed. Bindweed barred corners.

The garden she inherited had been taken
  by numerous apparitions, numberless,
    numbing, and humming autumn

  "Left alone in those warm rains
  her hair would grow dank"

II

Her self is never
recognized, but represented
impermanently and realistic
movement, another imitation.

Evening waves darkened   (Those constant travelers
the Lavender Princess's sleeves.   crash against cliffs,
foaming,

                  and reforming
boulders by their tales)
She had grown taller, more beautiful
from the gathering of far-off sights.

Now that the past is done, it stands
before us as though it were today.

Nor would she remember to bring it wrapped in rice paper to the
  meadow. Always elusive as day lilies,

Oh! what a sad plight, lost amid dream, shaking, shaking.

How does one exit such a story?
Stay with us awhile and maybe
the situation will look different.

FIREFLIES AND SUMMER RAIN

I

It is the Sixth Month and Malevolent Gods
are concealed under her goose feather pillow.

She will not be one of those unfortunates
who lives too long (always the adolescent dreams

of short life) but will form into the whirring of wings
or dew on shallow eaves or the privacy a young girl requires.

In the old stories, the Lavender Princess took courage.
Her low spirits

   "Guided by the moon
   An errant spirit"

And air warmed from the stirrings of Martin bells.

II

       Dewflower, Dragonflower

       May-beetle, Tigerbeetle

Certain *dai* lead from this world to the next.

          A strain on the koto. The hollow
          of her clavicle impressed
          by the closeness of music,
its spider web
          of sound, invisible and captivating

The devil's rival
Field Music

Tomorrow she will forget how enamored she was, taken by the concert
   of chirrups
and peaking blooms

(sounds music words)

Monkey music

III

She, the Lavender Princess, hidden behind a screen
                    so the young prince could allude to her

scent and shadow.

He, not allowed the briefest glimpse during his diurnal
                  amusements, amassed paintings of brilliant

color to excite sense.

In her pillow book she writes:

Good days, bad days—simply days,
morning & night—more days.
Regard the light! How it projects
a visual voice of god, and bouquets
of breath rise off wild grasses,
like Bodhisattvas.

An omen
we are not forgotten.

Mei-mei Berssenbrugge

New Form

That particular conjunction of events which includes the history of your body, your experience, and your art vertically, and the time and circumstances you are in horizontally, seeks an expression that is inevitably unique, or new.

A formal problem or limit represents a limit of what you can make or say or see at a particular moment. You might make a new form by following a desire or an intuition into a further, more contemporary part of you, such as varying the line length according to the horizon, embedding scientific terms into an equivocal or into a lyric context, using thought imagistically.

I find the idea of newness interesting, during a time when there is no recognized critical aesthetic. Criticism is at the edge of what it can discern or say, and so it's interesting to seek emerging form in fashion, in the margins of the arts, on the street, in experimental physics.

I have an intuition of a new form, as a new expertise in the topology of expression, emotion, and culture.

At first I characterized this new form by an idea of the horizontal, a horizontal cut across experience and culture, synchronistically and democratically, rather than the familiar vertical cut into tradition and essence.

But now I want to say it is a topological section or point of view, which could then include both verticals and horizontals along a complexity of a continuous surface, and with a new set of formal dynamics.

It's something which might take collage further.

It's my intuition about an aesthetic, or perhaps an intuition about a poem, and would require a new craft or form, analogous to the invention of a mathematics of surfaces.

It's an aesthetic I've noticed in younger or "newer" writers that is just beyond my grasp. I have an urge to understand what they know that enables them to generate this ungraspable form, and it is an urge from the intuition which desires a way to express convolutions of experiences and meanings in me, which are somehow all rising into a present tense, or tense of one time, or one surface.

It could be a way to write a poem across fragmented concentrations, for example, if you are raising children, instead of traditionally pursuing a single line. It could be a way to write a poem that responds to the barrage of layered stimuli in the world.

A friend tells me that, when she sees a deer next to a rock on a far hill, she learned as a child, by concentrating, to make the deer appear larger and closer, and the rock to diminish. When I ask a Yupik boy how he finds an animal on empty tundra, he tells me, you just look for the animal, until you see the animal.

The scientific notion of color as wavelengths of light—that we have in the light on our hands all possible colors—may not be true if you can call memory into being using a color. We can imagine a person inventing a color, now, seeing it for the first time, and that that new color's entrance pertains to a new appropriateness in the environment for it to be seen, not a predisposition.

This could be how a new form takes place.

———————

p.s. It's interesting for me to see that this essay written twenty years ago still accords with my ideas about poetry. Today I might replace the word "topological" with "holographic," because I meant both surface and implication.

Rabbit, Hair, Leaf

I

Some child left the cage unlatched
and George's rabbit hopped out with timid interest
while they were all inside eating cake
drank from the acequia where they found prints
and got its throat torn by a dog tame enough not to eat it
Their own dogs were lapping crumbs from plates
The rabbit with the velvet nose was only one he loved
because it was gentle like him, but others, too
more responsive though less like clouds were slaughtered
or died of their hearts: birds, a turtle who hibernated
too long. He still stares at chickadees scrabbling
on the snow-patched earth and wonders if he could love one
His most sensuous dreams are of a golden horse

2

Hair scattered on bare dirt
where an old woman has combed it
instead of going straight and smooth keeps falling
and the flesh that holds it keeps letting go
what isn't pecked away by coal-colored birds
or dragged a small distance by the coyote eating hair and all
The tiny tail-bone I found on a hill
bleached and tapered as a rat's nose
or that big fist of cow thigh by the cottonwoods
has nothing to do with the cloud we stepped through
accidentally, or the quick breath at the back of our necks
It is the animal in you smells death
though the real smell has gone to sage
that makes you start to run, but the ghost in you
makes you stay on that tenuous patch
of meadow fog on dirt. Eerie there are no bones
only white hair thick as milkweed
and big as a man with arms spread
so clean and old most of what's eaten it
likely dead, too

3

I picked up some yellow leaves you bled on
and put them in a book
I always thought the body died slowly
letting go as much as it understood at a time
Angry as you were in a minor way, it went to dirt
growing into something, with any water at all
But a dead horse in the stream, eyes gone
fouls what flows through it

Fog

I

Hundreds of millions of years ago, days were many hours shorter.

All things, sounds, stories and beings were related, and this complexity
was obvious. It was not simplified by ideas of relationship in one person's
mind.

Paths of energy were forced to stay in the present moment by being free
of references, making it impossible to focus on two things at once, and
showing by its quietness that energy of attention is as much a source of
value and of turbulence as energy of emotion.

As lava burst from the ground to cover the planet, it also freed water,
which escaped as massive, billowing fog, a contradicting ambition of
consciousness to acquire impressions and retain strong feelings.

Fog is a kind of grounded cloud composed, like any cloud, of tiny drops
of water or of ice particles, forming an ice fog.

Since water is 800 times denser than air, investigators were long puzzled
as to why fogs did not quickly disappear through fall-out of water
particles to the ground.

It turns out that the drops do fall, but in fog creating conditions, they
are buoyed up by rising currents or they are continually replaced by new
drops condensing from water vapor in the air.

Their realism is enhanced by smoothing away or ignoring discontinuities in the fog, for images of what we really see when we travel. Beautiful, unrepeatable, fleeting impressions can be framed only within the contradicting ambition of her consciousness to acquire impressions and to retain her feeling, a way of repeating a dream.

Large areas of the sky change from totally transparent to nearly opaque within a few minutes, although throughout a lifetime, the night sky appears remarkably constant.

Showing what they are without revealing what they are, paths of energy are transformed at the moment before their dissemination into an empty field, like dew you see on a spider web when the sun hits it, after there were spiders.

2

There is a great wall in the fog and rain.

There are some mountains in the mist.

There is the line of a wall in the mist. I go in and out of the fog on the rim trail, and the mountains rise in fog among yellow leaves.

There is a veil of fog between her and a sunlit flank of yellow leaves.

Slow whirling galaxies allow stars and gas to fall into hot disks of matter, orbiting around massive holes at the centers of the galaxies, allowing a branch to spring up at the moment when the snow melts from it.

Your concentration is interrupted by a shadow on the periphery of your memory of her.

Your concentration is a large array; where debris in the mind appears as an intense shower of heat radiation, like a cluster of instincts to the body.

3

As far as the transparency or relative compression of her boundaries is concerned, and your backward focus to it:

A white glass of water is hard to conceive of, because we cannot depict how the same thing would be white and clear, and how this would look.

She doesn't know what description these words demand of her, since she is alone.

She can sometimes see the events of a story as if they lay behind a screen, and it were transparent, rather like a sheet of glass, since human beings can be reflected on a smooth white surface in such a way that their reflections seem to lie behind the surface, and in a certain sense are seen through it.

4

She can describe for you the phenomenon of feeling her way through the fog. For whom does she describe this?

What ignorance can her description eliminate?

Which person is supposed to understand her description, people who have been lost in fog before, or people who have lived on the desert and never seen what she would describe?

You can be trying to connect the experience of being lost with something external or physical, but we are really connecting what is experienced with what is experienced.

So, when she tries to talk about the appearance of the people's feelings around her, she wants to connect how it appears to her with what is solid around her, but

she can connect appearance with appearance, how people *seem* to feel, and their communicating with each other within this appearance, from one person to another.

Is it possible for four different people in this way to have four different spatial concepts within the crowd? Somewhat different ones? Different with respect to one or another feature or heat inside a building, such as armspan or eye contact, and that could impair their mutual understanding to a greater or lesser degree? But often hardly at all, like ice broken up on the sea.

From above, I can't tell what distance away it is.

5

It has no shape or color that is stable, as if I had fallen asleep and a long bridge appeared, where my relatives are like companions crossing a bridge.

Her friends and family are like people you meet at the marketplace.

When you look at your husband, you think of a floating flag of the roof.

Even though he is your husband, he is not stable. Anyone believes what anyone says about you.

This is a realm or field in which other people exist in subtler forms than the body in daylight. A part of the person can become visible at a time, or parts of the people, and other parts rest in folds of the fog, as if they were muffled sounds.

It would be hard for you to believe that anything within the cloud exists.

His body, which you do not see exists, having dissolved its cells into a body of a cloud, which shifts in and out of focus.

It would not decay.

The body is the space of the point of a moment in your seeing him or hearing him.

You can calm yourself by moving toward one of these points, the way you move along your own breath.

6

You could try to make some fog into a piece of white cloth. This is impossible. Though it is visible, it is not a concrete substance. She tried to make a delicate cloud into a cloth. She could not, so that is why he is staying here.

Or, she could try alternating dissolving in the light with dissolving in the dark, for speed.

At night, she could see as if the country were illuminated, as if it were day. She could see each person's face clearly and she could remember if she had ever known this person before.

Dreams cannot disturb the fog or you, because your environment has no territory. There is no territory in a fog environment.

7

Lack of clarity within your environment is tormenting. It is felt as shameful. We feel we do not know how to even out a place for ourselves, where we should know our way about. But we get along very well inside buildings, without these distinctions, and without knowing our way about the decrepit structures.

In any serious interaction between them, not knowing your way about extends to the essence of what is between them. What can appear emotional is caused by the emission of energy out of her body, which you feel, but there is also such a thing as "feeling something as luminous,"

thinking of him as the color of polished silver or nickel, or a scratch in these metals.

8

This fog in space and light and dark is analogous to the solid ice of a very pure environment, and how it cracks and gets water, from one stage to another.

Its area of wide space varies in lightness from place to place, but does it look foggy to her in the darker places? The shadow that a cloud casts is in part darker. She sees the parts of the space that are farther away from the light as darker, but still white, even though she would have to add black to depict it.

Looking around in her room or any wide space in the evening, she can hardly distinguish among the people around her, and now becomes physically frightened of them.

And now, illuminate the space and describe each one you saw in the mist.

There are pictures of dreams in rooms in semi-darkness, but how can she compare the people in these pictures to those she saw in semi-darkness?

9

The bright light slows the senses. A picture of the space in bright light, as if etched by a laser, can slow your sense.

When we see or experience something with the senses and the senses get slowed, we can stop at this object, for example, a person who is beautiful.

As soon as we see this person, perception is blocked by the desire to go towards the person, with the misunderstanding of fog as thought, that just runs on and on. Her awareness is completely lost in distracting clearings of space.

10

The sky, which illuminates everything we see, can be gray. This can be true of someone around you in your family. How can she tell merely by its or his appearance that gray isn't itself luminous?

Thinking of him as the color of polished silver or other metal.

The fog of the way we feel our way into this focus, seeking by feeling, lies in the indefiniteness of the concept of continuing focus, or distance and closeness, that is, of our methods of comparing densities between human beings.

Is foggy that which conceals forms? And does fogginess conceal forms because it obliterates light and shadow, the way light obliterates or shadow obliterates, also?

Black does, but fog doesn't necessarily take away the luminosity of a color.

Darkness is not called a color.

11

The first solution that occurs to us for the problem of the appearance of another person is that ideas of actual feeling, instead of the appearance of feeling refer to points of tiny intervals or patches in the other person.

How are we to compare the feelings between two such intervals, simply by letting one's memory move from one to the other? If you do this to me, if you remember me, how do we know this feeling has not changed in the process? If you do remember correctly, how can we compare the feeling without being influenced by what has happened since?

The way we call a complex of intervals with which you depict the family member, his emotion with respect to you. As if the person were a piece of rose-colored glass.

Would he have the same emotion in a crowd as a piece of rose-colored paper?

A storyline develops based on your moving from one breath to another, and you start to want to continue it, like a span of good health or exceptional beauty. You want to continue it forever, and your memory gets involved, in how you perceive the space around you and the human beings or descendents in the space.

You will eventually feel so empty inside, among your family and in your memory of your family, that even while you continue breathing, your breath will not bring volume or space into your lungs.

12

They counted her more accurate and more inaccurate memories as black and white stones.

The more accurate memories turned out to be white on the outside, but they were unconditioned by the desire to form story out of her memory, continuing story, the way we wish this space and light to continue.

Therefore, we appreciate the fog, as the power to make the space continue beyond the single perception, into raw material or youth of the body, like a body of light.

It dissolves now at the top of her head, now five lights into her heart. Now, it dissolves into her body. Her friends dissolve into light. They dissolve into her family, which seems to dissolve into clouds that were already full of light.

It is not so much the quality or brightness of light, or her understanding of this light, as the number of times she dissolves. The faster she can dissolve into the space, the better.

It is almost as if the complete dark would be ideal.

Tan Tien

As usual, the first gate was modest. It is dilapidated. She can't tell
which bridge crossed the moat, which all cross sand now, disordered with footsteps.
It's a precise overlay of circles on squares, but she has trouble locating
the main avenue, and retraces her steps in intense heat for the correct entrance,
which was intentionally blurred, the way a round arch can give onto a red wall,
far enough in back of the arch for sun to light it.

If being by yourself separates from your symmetry, which is
the axis of your spine in the concrete sense, but becomes a suspension
in your spine like a layer of sand under the paving stones of a courtyard
or on a plain, you have to humbly seek out a person who can listen to you,
on a street crowded with bicycles at night, with their bells ringing.

And any stick or straight line in your hand can be your spine,
like a map she is following in French of Tan Tien. She wants space to fall
to each side of her like traction, not weight dispersed within a mirror. At any time,
an echo of what she says will multiply against the walls in balanced,
dizzying jumps like a gyroscope in the heat, but she is alone.

Later, she would remember herself as a carved figure and its shadow on a blank board,
but she is her balancing stick, and the ground to each side of her is its length,
disordered once by an armored car, and once by an urn of flowers at a crossing,

because Tan Tien is a park, now. The stick isn't really the temple's bisection around her, like solstice or ancestor. This Tang Dynasty peach tree would be a parallel levitation in the spine of the person recording it.

Slowly the hall looms up. The red stairway's outline gives way to its duration as it extends and rises at a low angle.
In comparison to the family, the individual hardly counts, but they all wait for her at a teahouse inside the wall.
First the gold knob, then blue tiers rise above the highest step, the same color as the sky.

When one person came to gain its confidence,
she imagines he felt symmetry as flight after his fast among seven meteorites in the dark. He really felt like a globe revolving within a globe.
Even the most singular or indivisible particle or heavenly sphere will adjust when the axis extending beyond itself is pushed, or the sphere it is within is pushed. What she thought was her balance flattens into a stylized dragon on the marble paving stones.

Yet she's reluctant to leave the compound. Only the emperor could walk its center line. Now, anyone can imagine how it felt to bring heaven news. She is trying to remember this in Hong Kong as the tram pulls suddenly above skyscrapers and the harbor and she flattens against her seat, like a reversal occurring in the poles, or what she meant by, no one can imagine how.

Safety

Increasingly in our world, forgiveness is asked for, granted, withheld, face-to-face or below the surface, like slow combustion, and I need to elucidate the chain of oxidation.

You fill around the open space of our being here, tensile welds, not empty in the sense, a weld yields.

The pathetic story is removed from calculation.

Yet, banality in identifying with others is no cause for pathos to dissolve.

So, I continue to calculate my house, its significance as a holding place for something to look at (image, word), building would illustrate.

I saw, when a building falls, interior remains interior.

Then, individuals acquire that same size.

Also, the innateness of being a witness annexes size, by seeing putting you next to.

I mean, immense size.

One folds in and re-opens to outside, not *as if* building for someone afraid of heights, who strains long, structural tresses of light, trying to wear out an image.

Safety

The photograph is handsome of the young man.

Points of likeness puncture the surface of my sight, absent person I bring inside from the interior he inhabits as friend, i.e., innate, strange, as artificial light.

Neighbor by neighbor, a composition not inscribed in framed space, now haunts it.

Piece comes from you (referent) in me, safe house for the virtual as possible, with unlocatable brightness and clarity.

Ground is the beginning, how I remember you by its lack of a basis on which to found, instant replay, afterimage hollowed out in advance, your family who feels secure, their voices.

Don't be afraid to see something you don't want to see.

What if the beginning has no motion, just size, height?

Follow this line.

Your fear of coming to the end is relieved, when you look back through its hollowness.

You see receding x's, joints, (forever) connect the line to its interior (witness), as what fills a space, what arcs it away?

Safety

Urban space is a series of partial views, convex, opaque.

You go from mass to detail, individuals, little ants.

The instinct to preserve oneself deflects onto vertigo from the domination of space, fear of death to fear of damage to the beautiful body.

You connect dwelling to a child guarded by a woman.

Its fate is foretold, child implicit in a word-chain, flash, flowers in ice.

In the days we have left, we count our probable meetings, first surface content, then in your language, as in my dream.

The more disconnected your monologue, the more it correlates to something latent in that moment, separation, flowers in ice.

It's not raining, but it's as if there were mud everywhere, and you're plastered in mud.

When a person falls in front of you, something like rain washes mud away, and his leg becomes white as a piece of marble.

Being with each other, we want to reveal and reveal, conceal nothing, but there's the sense something does not get across, a secret.

In this sense, hospitality between us is a secret interior, instead of reality being the plaintiff's.

Shards, detail, singularity, winter garden in glass, palms, extreme refinement of the civility.

There's a linking of structure, joint and weld, a springiness, and an unlinking across expanse.

The rigor of the link is an artifact.

Its volume is innate in the witness, leg covered over, memorialized by what I saw, concealed, closed, covered with sight as with gauze, light surface with which I wrap you, light trampoline.

Gillian Conoley

I try to think of my poetics as a highly protean thing. Language is protean, poetry is protean. One has to be willing to throw oneself into a sort of bottomless, bubbling cauldron for the work to be vital. The writers and painters and other artists I admire most are the ones who were working artists all their lives, who reserved the right to change at any moment, and did, who were most attracted to their art because of the kind of boundless, procreative state of being that art demands. Highly set-in-stone poetics scare me; they seem limiting and fascistic, ponderous and dull. Having said that, I do have many ideas about poetry that have been my steadfast though mercurial companions. I look to poetry to fill me with the transrational, with a kind of counter-logic to take me beyond my own habits of thought or perception; to challenge the obvious or the apparent; to multiply meaning; to take me beyond whatever it is I may think that I am writing or thinking. If poetry instructs us, it instructs us beyond the obvious. Poetry is a critique and a resistance to the obvious. It opens new pathways to perception, and never rests there, exclaiming "this is the way to see the world!" The nature of reality, the nature of the individual, is not fixed, nor is poetry. Language is not a vehicle for preexistent meanings but is an unwieldy gloriously impossible system through which meaning can often pass, often profoundly, but never completely rest, though certainly one can find long and measured moments, as in rests in music. Language is material, and it is the material of human consciousness, and human consciousness is its material: recognizable, even comfortable, but mysterious, peculiar, unknowable. Even Wittgenstein couldn't decide which cart before which horse. While all this is decidedly postmodern of me, there is a touch of the old-fashioned in my work as well. I love narrative, though I am not a narrative poet. I love the enchantment of the tale, the mysterious spell one falls under in the telling of the story. It's the whole story I don't particularly trust. I love allegory, the deep layering of soils, the sturdy ground of skeletal underpinnings allegory constructs, no matter how uncertain the telling of the tale may be. Allegory should never be too a-to-b-to-c, however, never too sure of what it is actually allegorical of, or things get too reductive. Allegory should perhaps be more like some misplaced bone sticking out of the wrong grave. Languages break down as people break down. Poetry is not something one writes, poetry is something one attends to. Poetry is social, in that language is social, in that humans are social, and it has a social force.

The Birth of Beauty

Drained by combat, the amorous were elsewhere, so that home, chasm, it was immaculate. An hour without brothers or sisters, only a dove holding a ring. That morning Death woke up not a cricket, not a boy burying his toy pistol, but a mother, that woman in a black wig entering the swan-drawn car. And in all manner of words or shapes, on either hand stars grew for us. When lakes, ponds, swimming pools drained the invisible, men walked into mirrors. The woman's lap opened, riding the black border between the worlds, a shuddering leaping of one form into another. A lemon grove metallic against the blue sky. Apple tossed without bite, a rose that took a name for all our impossible love.

We Don't Have to Share a Fate

We don't have to share a fate,
we don't have to draw shameful conclusions.

After the shutter releases,
I want you in the plural,

in the snake carriage,
in the glacier room,

in the closet full
of guitars and stomped hay,

in the exhalation of others,
all swaying with love, but changing midway

through the words
I address to you, my hand

pressed to yours visibly
much paler

than before, an orchid
offered beneath a warring sky,

an orchid that yawns
and cracks open and falls apart

unexpected in a bed of soft clothes,
where your shoulders became two steps,

dawns fruits rivers and knives,
full glottal, wide lens

and your hands became two countries,
and my legs murmured like grass,

a dumb love,
a tether to all dreams of enduring,

long convoy between two powers
killing the mockery of words

while daylight floats,
orchids, white dogs stretched out between the slow-burning lanterns.

Flute Girl

I kept coming in whenever anyone else entered,
like the drunk man,

or behind
Socrates, a sudden opening

like quick-grabbing an extra newspaper off
someone else's coin

    before the latch shuts,
or the soft hush of the ATM card as it enters—

these are sounds
you may know intimately.

Love a silver reed.
Between the teeth.

    Some words
creaked
coming out of the rhetoric—

I was sent away.
Back into the opening.
    The blur on the other side
where I'm hidden
    though not exactly
stricken,
    beautiful and silent so that I may be lacking—

This is
what made me

    audible to you.

Alcibiades

A boy at table   comes a man in cloak

a leg seems   a light discrete

a wrong door, a wrong door,   some wake

if he   had loved me   his talk would not have been

almost   the talk of a god

blankets between us   too earthly

breath   the off-green of new grapes

love   exchanging itself for words   is like

kissing your sister   kissing your older brother when you sleep

Socrates

Predictably Socrates is late to the seminar on Socrates.

He is too at hotel with himself,

a place in his voice no sound comes through,

opposite of evangelist.

Like a situation in his dreams in which he couldn't.

All this could happen,
even to Mr. For Whom the Birds Must Stop Singing.

For us, too, so a feeling is changing, and soon   it's cut here,

what dawn is this
     humans tumbling

and the star hanging

enchant as neon interrupts to rose.

No one can know what is wanted.
Before it all starts flowing into a different emotion.

Inelegant Motherless Child

Inelegant motherless child appears

actually on the impenetrable roadsides

Wind, shack   and roadside   Flag

lifting abstraction

lifting gravel from abstraction: pretty wild.

Wild that this   stays America, episodic are the genuflections.

You can pay
to pay attention. It is impossible

though
inelegant being: I see you plainly in the alley.   Outside.

My atrocity acquaints your atrocity
we're sitting on a stoop.

The American People
stopping to drink juice at the impenetrable roadsides.

The shore lapping in

The boatman appearing
as a guide figure in a dream,

"I can get you to Jersey."

I don't know about you,
but I want to be here.

This is the life

My imaginary thumb

in the air
to your imaginary thumb

we are both shot in the back with an arrow.

This is the life,

how it feels inside you

                         civic   unruly

neither nor,   nary

the old haunts

you are paid to represent

murmurous then

                         piercingly settled

                         exhaustion of the mind

I see you plainly in the alley

stick-figured

drawing

scratched among dim shapes into the

back of a chair

Native

Let me see
if I can understand you as part of the architecture

though it is the architecture of the place

that keeps killing me, dream of sky that stays
perfect blue foam, dream unfurling

gone and fusing like a hand that has fallen
into place.

You are at the pond

and the beach and over the want ads

and then I have the quieter
impulse to paint
beneath envy's carriage
along eternity's mill.

Earth kicking me up in the form of the human,

and taking the meaning
and giving back the meaning

as the photographs do with the life.

Before rheumy eyes
before young strapping eyes.

A mystery you didn't step over
the white painted hot dog stand

dwarf autumn marigold

a gold chain to look, and look away.

To looky here lies your
empty leg, your empty leg of even gin I would give you

for just the hint of I
I essence
I nuance up the flue.

For the rheumy eyes
For the young strapping eyes.

And begin bicycling a side road in the gaping jaws of

sweet anthem that plays
but follows like murder like entropy like lassitude,

a shade, and then a plain, and then a majesty.

Abandoned on the shore

                a red towel,

            oh my automaton odalisque.

The sun and the wind and the resultant white cloud

then the car gone off in yellow traffic like a "so there"

might we have in conversation,

as in who am I   to write this, who

Who   who is speaking   most whoever-ly,

Who, you are pale

though always

you are social.

As ever,   it is water from a spring

to walk with you

Kathleen Fraser

In a recent comment re: the magnetic force that Ludwig Wittgenstein has long held for writers & artists, Terry Eagleton paraphrases the essayist David Schalkwyk, who connects Wittgenstein, in his permanent refugee status, to the philosophical project of "leading erring words patiently back to their homes."

His perspective highlights a prominent task—and temptation—for the poet compelled by the disorder and reordering of language as it invites us to comb through it, as if it were ours to bring into line or to reinvent . . . *and it is.*

Wittgenstein's foregrounding of the term "investigation" in his *Philosophical Investigations* sets forth a *practice* of coming to the world without certainty, but rather with curiosity, *un*belonging to an established ordering, an openness to ambiguity and the unfinished . . . even the untried.

In my own practice as a poet, since the early 1960s, my path has been marked by a great deal of trial and error as I pulled away from innocently acquired traditional musics and the ecstatic readiness of my English-marked childhood texts, eventually swerving away from the familiar and reassuring "known" towards difficulty: American *voice* as it was delivered to me in urban jazz; the new music of Cage and his followers; the playful, celebratory, and concealed mysteries of New York School poetries

(O'Hara and Guest, in particular); and the more compressed severity found in the Objectivist voices of Oppen, Niedecker, and Bunting.

However, the impact of the visual arts as practiced in the '60s in New York City was entirely rearranging my spatial sense of canvas and page, and while I did not consciously recognize this until much later, the poetics and practice of Charles Olson's open-field, full-page graphics—his archeological models for layering and "digging"—were creating a kind of visual permission that would begin to find articulation in my work, particularly from 1980 forward, when I had time away from full-time teaching and could spend regular periods in Italy—especially, Rome—where the continuous presence of *physical* history, in its layers of disintegration and reconstruction, became part of my daily life and a powerful model for how I wanted to work . . . to be able to imbed the fragments of the physical world around me, as well as its *heard* bi-linguality, into the visual body of the poem.

This became my way of responding to the pollution of speech and thought that threatens from every quarter—dismantling seductive writing habits via the peripheral vision of investigation, and intentionally constructing works marked by hidden error and the daily imperfections of the crowded, pruned, glued, re-written, disappeared history I walk through into unexpected paste-ups.

. . . "leading erring words patiently back to their homes."

Medusa's hair was snakes. Was thought, split inward.

I do not wish to report on Medusa directly, this variation of her writhing. After she gave that voice a shape, it was the trajectory itself in which she found her words floundering and pulling apart.

Sometimes we want to talk to someone who can't hear us.
Sometimes we're too far away. So is a shadow
a real shadow.

When he said "red cloud," she imagined *red*
but he thought *cloud* (this dissonance in which she was feeling
trapped, out-of-step, getting from here to there).

Historical continuity
accounts for knowing what dead words point to,

a face staring down through green leaves as the man looks up
from tearing and tearing again at his backyard weeds. His red dog sniffs
at what he's turned over. You know what I mean.
We newer people have children who learn to listen as *we* listen.

M. wanted her own.
Kept saying *red dog. Cloud.*
Someone pointing to it while saying it. Someone discovering stone.

Medusa trying to point with her hair.
That thought turned to venom.
That muscle turning to thought turning
to writhing out.

We try to locate blame, going backwards.
I point with my dog's stiff neck
and will not sit down,
the way that girl points her saxophone at the guitar player
to shed light
upon his next invention. He attends her silences, between keys,
and underscores them with slow referents.

Can she substitute *dog* for *cloud,* if *red* comes first?
Red tomato.
Red strawberry.

As if all of this happens on the ocean one afternoon in July,
red sunset soaking into white canvas. The natural world.
Darkness does eventually come down.
He closes her eye in the palm of his hand.
The sword comes down.

Now her face rides above his sails, her hair her splitting tongues.

Flashes of light or semaphore waves, the sound
of rules, a regularity from which the clouds drift
into their wet embankments.

Notes re: Echo

SEPTEMBER 4

The sunset again, a favorite time of the horizon he might wish to play out.

Less than what was meant, as a last point of resistance, then its answer or echo or next.

It could be in the identification of spectrum order. A color which didn't include red. Or, if one had the temperament, all the possible red categories.

Values of red.

*

Coffee takes its immediate effect; a system had been registering its blur. Things were not right. "Not quite," he said.

The holidays and their deliberate, agonizingly habitual tables. Too much animal fat. Beef ribs and lamb ribs in succession, in sauces with equally talented cooks. Focus on the gesture and an appropriate "ummmm good" dissevers him from a clear path that had achieved a balance he now took for granted in the wake of hiccups.

SEPTEMBER 5

That pressure behind you pushing with increasing lightness, the beginning of September, the fourth, at noon, exactly, and all the news falling out of your little cubbyhole, smelling of cheap purple ink. Interpretations now. Messages from me to you. A room of faces looking for the good, the true and the beautiful.

Plan 1: Wearing a slit skirt will divert their expectations

Plan 2: The decision not to eat an apple in front of them.
Intimacy retrieved. Laying down the law. Putting a boundary between us:

All of you are (A). I, alone, am (B). But we share this perception and, in that, we all are (C), together, filled with anticipation of the future.

Plan 3: Here is my syllabus.

SEPTEMBER 6

Elements of disorder. A sweet disorder in the dress. The idea of order in Key West. Disorder and Early Sorrow. Order me a beer.

SEPTEMBER 7

Dear Narcissus,

Is language, in fact, the pool? Looking into your words as if they represented a surface of water (Narcissus gazes with longing, trying to find himself), do I then find me, a word I know? Yes. No. Some deflection, in-flexing of where we might overlap. Sitting on your lap, a word comes back at me, as an echo. So I divest myself of the disembodied me . . . Echo is She who watches Narcissus look for himself and returns him to himself, slightly altered, by her very attentiveness.

Where am I?
Love,
Echo

SEPTEMBER 8

The echo is blunt-eared. Narcissus blundered.
"You are really gone."   "This is really school."

*

"What makes you most anxious about this class?"

One woman wrote, "I am afraid that what I want to say will not be important enough."

On reading this statement, another woman remarked: "You could drop that part. We're really beyond that."

SEPTEMBER 9

What you admire unequivocally and love wholeheartedly is not mine.

SEPTEMBER 10

Dear Narcissus,

While you were gone, I divided into two even more distinct territories.

*

Walking up to a new edge, I discovered in myself an old mute. But I stayed, allowing my curiosity to teethe on the silence. A hope for mutation? A belief in mutability. It was, of course, a question of language. Of a code shared by the interior of four fingers and a thumb who knew each other's openings and closings. Knew how to make a fist, the form of which I recognized and hated, while feeling an odd affection and curiosity for each of the parts.

In what appeared to be home, I was also alone. I missed our talks, which always pull me somewhere new, but in your friendly red wagon with its creaky wheels. So I began to write about my grandfather, who was out-of-order, displaced from his known function and terrain. These stories were written within a solid and digested tradition of linked sentences. Achieving their life gave me a kind of satisfaction I'd not known.

Why, then, do I trust your language enough to enter it? I trust it because it is both watchful and fluid, allowing the variants of yourself to have voice. Am I who you hear?

Love,
Echo

SEPTEMBER 11

His words. How they tone up, then polarize or identify certain pleasures. Activate some as yet unexercised part. But the beautiful surface is always involved with seduction. And what of the darker, colder water? One cannot deny its pull.

How, then, to hold on to the *who* you think you are. The image in water shifts, according to the light's impact, and currents we cannot wholly predict.

It's always were.

And we are sifting. We are the foggy morning's gray shape moving . . . and beyond the bridge, nothing but clear blue skies.

*

"Echo watches over her shoulder on another rock on the other side of the stream, resigned, as Narcissus is constantly on the way, surprised."

—*for Steve Benson*

Claim

Claim through and through,
breathe me now window.

Lift. Oh turn your back.
Turn will do

where no words fall
in the clearing we make.

What light still flickers out
of history glamorous?

Gibberish, self-pity
slams books to the floor

with curses. In several dresses
the dark weeds repeat

their occupancy. Enemy
season alerts these

skeletons. Listening mind,
mine. Rosy genitals

regret your hiding manifold,
those fine-creased boundaries,

longing muscle,
my spoon, your face

between away
and a clearing. You were

this place made of nothing,
sniffing around. Four legs,

meadow animal, trees
called into hearing.

Losing people

Upon us white.
Open white and fall

and finally break
through late November

and strain where snow
did gather its weight

to childhood and the body.
Shifts accelerate

from a loud street,
tires where leaves rub

little at ourselves.
A day inside, gazing long

from the sea. We name it
blanket or dark.

Those labdabum hours

You couldn't find it in the bird's weight
pulling an arc through the twig. You must

catch yourself somewhere or fall anywhere.
Four cherries, red showing through

green webs. This surprise may not catch you
and that is the trouble. A whole new life

may be just another tree. Now the floor
is as clean as vinegar. It shines

from rubbing. Sleeping inside your little
and constant coughs, you could hear

someone helping you, finally waking.
The helper has her rags and tools.

With tenacity she hangs on to the dimming
vision. You are trying too hard

to enter this world. The door is open.
What can you find in this

that is yours, wholly? A belief,
not to be divided into silken strands

in air. This childish hope. I give you up,
each day, to another. Abstract acts

of generosity, as we dream in two positions
on the bed, with the softer, lighter pillows

just under our heads, some slight elevation.
Whole sentences are subtracted from

conversation. Darkness moves continuously
behind that line where the sun presses.

To let go of shapes held in peaches,
the bruise of a thumb and forced sweetness.

You were the lightest of all the silver-white metals.

You can hear her breathing in the photograph

What causes a person—say, in a family—to feel he or she is different than
the other members, separate, an extra bit of jigsaw puzzle with unreliable
hump, listing to one side of the table after the entire cardboard picture
lies perfect and flat?

Who, finally, complies and merges—at every point—with the agreed
upon shape of a human torso or preferred community type? Is arrival
focused by admirable intention or by an off-camera genetic predictor,
trapped just at the periphery of departure? Perhaps it is more like the
snapping back of a stretched rubber band to its inherent ovoid design?
(Even now I see my current favorite—wide, flat and intensely violet in
color—resisting an equal force designed to hold three stems of broccoli in
place, pulling away from and then returning to its familiar elastic function
closing in around them.)

And what of disruption, departure . . . even from something that lodges
so functionally within our grasp?

•

For instance, these opening lines—led by grammar and punctuation into
the promise of coherence. Now I must turn my back on them. Is it the
turning away that marks me? Is everyone else in my "family" looking
inward to a center, or are they also turning their gaze sideways? Do they
see the gray animal shadow whizzing along the floorboards? Do they hear

the parquet geometry of the wooden floor expanding, as if giving-up an hour of footsteps randomly wandering backwards, forwards?

•

Daphne is rushing into leaves. Her mouth is stretching sideways into the opposite of an expanded, purposeful plan. Bernini's chisel lingers inside Apollo's right foot; he's finally coaxed the marble of the left leg into a sprint, showing veins breaking through. But Daphne's traveling ahead of herself. *Why must the photograph of the two of them come out of its envelope every year and be pinned to the wallpaper?* A. still believes D. is the girl he thought she was and continues describing her to herself, even as tree bark is creeping between her thighs and pushing from roots that lift her body higher with the force of minute-by-minute growth.

•

They are two perfect bodies, entirely hard white marble caught in absolute dark. Bernini found the immense hunk of marble, brought down with ropes to the masonry yard near Pietrasanta. A wealthy man paid for the purchase of it, as in gaining on a dream that's left nothing in you but a mute feeling-around for something lost—another gamble of horses or dogs contested and persuaded into predatory sport.

Bernini works in marble without knowing what it may deliver. He's in love with the slow revelation of the chase: Apollo's concentration, Daphne's uneasiness. She's disappearing, he knows that much. *Apollo's claim of certainty should be gaining on her, shouldn't it?* You can hear her breathing in the photograph as it's unpinned from the wall and put away in a box, exposing the anatomy of imagined capture, even when you're not looking at it.

•

The museum photographer, noting the Villa's high windows, lights the bodies to catch the dramatic hollows of ribs and male trunk. But it is Daphne's eyes, sliding with the immense pull of gravity, that stop you . . . you have been taken by the hand and led to this.

Bernini has entered them. The photographer is talking to himself and shifts the armature of high-wattage lighting. *Apollo almost has her,* he thinks. *You can tell by his floating, unclenched hand and the conviction in his eyes as deep and particular as oxygen entering cell walls. He needs— what?—to stop her and to hold the thing he knows must be his, even though some part of him back there in the dark—and because of tracking her inside and outside of time—notices the tough green leaves, probably a kind of tree he doesn't recognize as local, and he's only just seen that they're sprouting, and not just from her hands.*

•

She did not think—or did she?—running towards herself and having no idea of where the next life might be. Out of sight seemed the place.

She was inside and outside of him and visible, forced too soon by his definiteness.

Her indefiniteness was not tolerable to his practiced will.

She wanted the shape of a lintel.

When Bernini chipped the final piece of stone from the block of marble, he saw what he'd done. But it was too late and he'd already turned away.

Forrest Gander

In *Torn Awake,* I was interested most in developing phrasal overlays and polyrhythms and then in driving them through suspensions and repetitions toward a complex emotional and intellectual experience. In *Eye Against Eye,* I've tried to speed up the longer poems, to find lyric rhythms that could evoke the multi-faceted, multi-vocal surge of the present. If the earlier poems are centrifugal, expansive in reference and register, I want the new ones to be centripetal, their energies pressing inward.

Why the difficulty, the dense passages?

I would say that my language is grounded in what Jan Zwicky calls "the essential lack of clarity in human experience attendant on the exercise of our capacity for language." Aristotle claimed that "not to have one meaning is to have no meaning," but ambiguity is essential to language and consciousness.

In my quotidian experience, my awareness alternately blurs and sharpens. In my poems, words turn opaque, textured as sound, pitch, rhythm, woven into design and then they come clear as meanings shaped by that design. I think we see them and we see through them. Texture and text. Nontransparent aesthetic form and transparent thematic content. It is this staging of transparence and density, of appearance and disappearance, which is, for me, the erotic tension in the work.

Of Torn Awake

I've wondered whether it is possible to find a line, syntax, rhythmical orchestration that would decentralize the subject's control of the sentence or, likewise, expand the range of agencies. As part of that investigation in reading, these poems have been nourished by Merleau-Ponty's *The Visible and the Invisible* and *The Phenomenology of Perception* and also by Levinas, Ricouer, Shusterman, and Henri Bergson.

In an earlier book, *Deeds of Utmost Kindness*, I tried to work out a lineal and thematic formalism from geology to write the poems of "The Blue Rock Collection." So, for instance, the poem called "Yellow Quartz" is composed in six lines and references the passage of light because quartz crystals are hexagonal and pellucid. Later, this came to seem arbitrary to me. An entertaining, Oulipoean practice, but overly determined.

In *Torn Awake*'s "Line of Descent," I wanted the poem to have the look and feel of that winding, cutting back, vertiginous (hence air on both sides) descent by foot into the Grand Canyon, and I was remembering, too, the clarity of the strata as you descend the steeper north face. Of course you read the stratigraphic layers as you descend, not only visually but like a Braille. It is impossible not to trace your fingers across the rocks, to feel the Triassic conglomerates shift into the Permian sandstones and shales and then into the Redwall limestones. The strata extend and thin out or are cut away, and sometimes there are abrupt uncomformities (which the form of the poem about father and son in the KOA bathroom means to enact—the visual unconformity parsing a geological feature into a metaphor for the psychological and emotional disconnection between parent and child). I wanted the line to take all that on.

In "The Hugeness of That Which is Missing," I'm responding to both a sense of personal loss for a close friend who died—"weeks after the [funeral] service, they open a letter"—and to the radioactive poisoning of the desert. But in the poem, I'm less interested in launching an argument than in allowing the sensual and meditative to interact, as I feel they do in my own actual exigent experience. I hope to provide an inherently different form of insight, one that may be incommensurable with rational analysis. So the poem's indeterminacy mirrors its thematic obsession with faith, belief, what can be known, how we might continue to feel each other when we are all so blasted, all but overcome by self-concern ("did I piss it away in talking" or "was it insignificant before I bent my gorgeous attention over it"), loss (of friendship, of faith in the "fixed point" of a controlling narrative, of hope), and media's corruption of language (mistranslation, the blur of events that dilute experience, equivocation, the turn of phrase that is a false step).

In "Voiced Stops": a language as stressed and baroque and emotionally torqued as the experience, my own anyway, of raising a child beyond all the myths of raising a child. Of being raised by a child.

In "Line of Descent" with geology and with "Carried Across" with the Spanish language, to incorporate into experience its literal strata—what we stand on as both figural and actual at once—and, in another place, the sound and image and the shifting metaphors of understanding that might begin to give an account of that place. I.e., to write of experience not as something proceeding from a subjectivity but penetrated by the world and others, entangled with corollary systems of meanings, layers of rhythm and voice and depth. To connect the human spirit to the significance of the world that harbors it.

Face

What lasts in thinking is not
So much the way
As its horizon, the plum side
Not facing us but richer
In contingency

        a lateral
Sheer rock wall
From which hiero-
Glyphs wave what
Lasts comes after
The red flash
The negative
Commemoration outside of
Syntax, human
Recognition turned away
From finally itself

to pinions, one seed
Junipers, scree
Blasted like rusty cans
The prehistoric wind blinds
Us with dust a cactus
Spine goes through our shoe
But we are bent
Upon not that

Field Guide to Southern Virginia

True as the circumference
to its center. Woodscreek Grocery,
Rockbridge County. Twin boys
peer from the front window, cheeks
bulging with fireballs. Sandplum trees
flower in clusters by the levee. She
makes a knot on the inside knob
and ties my arms up
against the door. Williamsburg green.
With a touch as faint as a watermark.
Tracing cephalon, pygidium, glabella.

*

Sway-back, through freshly cut stalks,
stalks the yellow cat. Can you smell
where analyses end, the orchard
oriole begins? Slap her breasts lightly
to see them quiver. Delighting in this.
Desiccation cracks and plant debris
throughout the interval. In the Black-
water River, fishnets float
from a tupelo's spongy root
chopped into corks. There may be sprawling
precursors, descendent clades there are none.

*

The gambit declined was less
promising. So the flock of crows
slaughtered all sixty lambs. Toward the east, red
and yellow colors prevail.
Praying at the graveside,
holding forth the palm of his hand
as a symbol of God's book.
For the entirety of the Ordovician.
With termites, Mrs. Elsinore explained,
as with the afterlife, remember:
there are two sides to the floor. A verb
for inserting and retrieving
green olives with the tongue. From
the scissure of your thighs.

*

In addition, the trilobites
were tectonically deformed. Snap-on
tools glinting from magenta
loosestrife, the air sultry
with creosote and cicadas.
You made me to lie down in a peri-Gondwanan back-arc basin.
Roses of wave ripples and gutter casts.
Your sex hidden by a goat's beard.
Laminations in the sediment. All
preserved as internal molds
in a soft lilac shale.

*

Egrets picketing the spines of cattle in fields edged
with common tansy. Flowers my father gathered
for my mother to chew. To induce abortion. A common,
cosmopolitan agnostoid lithofacies naked in the foothills. I love
the character of your intelligence, its character as well as pitch.
Border wide without marginal spines. At high angles
to the inferred shoreline.

*

It is the thin flute of the clavicles, each rain-pit
above them. The hypothesis of flexural loading. Aureoles
pink as steepleflower. One particular day, four hundred
million years ago, the mud stiffened
and held the stroke of waves. Orbital motion.
Raking leaves from the raspberries, you
uncover a nest of spring salamanders.

Anniversary

Not to be known always by my wounds,
I buried melancholy's larvae

And cleaved the air behind you.
Myself I gathered

Like the middle dusk
To the black tulips of your nipples.

For seven days we shut the door,
We scoured the room with birds' blood.

And for a little while
In the hollow where your throat rose

From between your splendid clavicles,
Our only rival was music,

The piano of bonewhiteness.
Nor did the light subside,

But deepeningly contracted.
The rawness of the looking.

The quiver.

Garment of Light

For two figures preserved at Pompeii

Before the hand stretches out to intensify time's discipline,
it accumulates a thickness, accretionary lapilli.
Horseshoe-shaped calderas gape toward the sea.
                                        The bridge begins
as an open chord. In the mountains, falls
are magmatic and subtle.
He does not know where to guide her eyes.
Before gigantic blocks shift
and transform into avalanche, before swifts mute
warm dung in their eyes:
small phreatomagmetic or scoriaceous or small
phreatic explosions, heavy ashfall and darkness for several days.

Where does she hide, now, his nervous, strange exhilaration?
When 3 is the tertiary slope and 6 is the crater rim?
                                    How do they go on
chewing words like crickets, if 8
is the landscape, and 10 is the town?
What will their children find to weigh the fire in?

At the tension beyond the opening, they unwrap their secret
voices of fine, bluish-gray pumice shards.
They, known now as consecutive numbers, following
each other to an extreme inner distance.

If lava were not derived of exigence,
the scarp might reveal a parasitic cone.
But volcanic glass hisses forth
carrying free plagioclase crystals. In quiet fumarolic
emissions, the glow faces their faces. Look,
they have scrawled
into the hatched tephra a word
half-obscured by mud
under which they lie. Our days
come tagged to that foreign
inscription, a delicate, enharmonic reply.

To C

Inside, inside the return, inside, the hero diminishes.
Over her vessel they place a veil, and when it is lifted
the name of the vessel has been lost. Consider
the darkness of the water which has no scent
and neither can it swallow. Yet the ship's bow
extends over the proscenium like a horse
at a fence and the orchestra stands and files out.
On the long walk home, I long to see your face.

To Eurydice

Like a man who watches from close, like a man
who watches from close the motion of a chorus, the slow
choreography back and forth, hypnotized, like that
man who goes home to drink his black water: I am.
As far as my perceptions refer to what we called
the real world, they are not certain. As far as they are certain
they do not refer to what we called the real.

I was there when you began to cheat on the high notes,
gobble lines for extra air. Even at that,
you floored me. The applause, smothering. I shivered
in a cold sweat. Smothering. And when I stepped
from the theater through the cordon of mounted police,
I saw myself upside-down in a horse's eye. Though I
was prepared, a place had yet to be prepared. I rode
the Tenryu ferry under a stand-and-wait moon.
I polished the statue with beeswax.

It's beginning to have a familiar ring, isn't it?
I've instructed myself to speak more slowly. As though
I were in a play.

I stepped from the theater. I kneeled,
kneeled before the statue. *The story has a skip in it.*

What is your distance but my impatience? Lichens live
under crusts of rock for a thousand years. I will never
condescend to be a mere object of turbulent
and decisive verbs. Is leaving whom? Has left whom?

It is not Orpheus speaking. Do you even know
who is speaking? Dear Eurydice. There was a rip in your stocking.
When the cry flashed across hills (*not your cry,*
but my own), no baffle could muffle it, every hiding place
clenched shut, and a spasm rolled out from me and over the field.
The given is given. How the past waxes fat! Overhead
is now below. There was a rip

in something. Here. No, here on this page.
Whose fingerprints are not smeared across the telling? That
third person beside you. That was my character. Il terzo incomodo.
I have instructed myself to speak more slowly. It is morning.
The fog draws back its thin lavender scent.

When I kicked off my shoes to carry you—*how could I guess*
it was the beginning of my concentration, a test—into
the cramped bedroom, a cross-marked spider crawled my foot.
Upon this intentionality another would impinge. But I
was soaked in pleasure's spittle and you
submitted your willing throat. Wailful. You were. You are.

It was later, later you met Orpheus. His wealth, his fame.
His girlish smile. He went to absurd lengths, he lied
solely to appear mysterious. He played you—
that dreary chorus wending back and forth behind him—
ridiculous *morna* songs for which we hooted him offstage,
but you swallowed it.

When the cry wrung itself from between my teeth. *What*
was the last word? Offstage? There is a sound caught
in my ears, a particular sound like the sound of a breath.
How did it go, the telling? Your face
stayed in the dirt as though you saw into it.

When the cry ricocheted from the hills and screwed

back into me, wasn't it my wakening? It was my castration. *Who is that
other one beside her, they asked. It is not Orpheus
speaking. Orpheus, used up in the rashness of his first impulse.*

What was torn away is speaking.

Like flakes struck from a stone ax. Like flakes
from a stone ax, the scales have fallen from my eyes
rendering me impervious to panic. Ploughed
and harrowed my soul is. And yet. (*The rip
is full of voices.*) I cannot stop this incessant scheming.
With what word, what gambit,
might a stubborn, remnant hope contract even further
and even further into a summons?

Ligature 5

For Valerie Mejer

It's not an insult to refuse to drain the glass, she tells me
And a fly crawls from the bowl of sauza picante.

Would you choose to bury the organs with the child?
And he retreats to his room and closes the door.

Here, birds in the zocalo whiz and tweet like children's toys
And there, a charred corpse hanging from the bridge.

From the seat behind, the boy pokes his sister's head with a plastic fork
And getting no response, tests it on his own head.

Would you turn the damn wipers off, the attendant asks
And the odor of manure and wet hay hits us.

A kind of mystery gloms to those who have suffered deeply
And thank you Mr. and Mrs. Radiance.

It sounded like the chimmuck of a rock dropped into a stream
And the piston-driven breathing of sex.

The couple at the bus station—when had we kissed like that?
And *Nice evening—Yes it is—A bit skunky—That's for sure.*

Terrorist and victim circling the last chair as the music stops
And the valves of their mouths snapping open and shut.

When I rise out of myself into occasion, I said
And when do you rise out of yourself into occasion, she asked.

Late enough to count maple loopers and geometrids at the window
And the boy will be coming up the porch steps when he comes.

The long row of treadmills choiring
And above them, televisions replay the disaster.

Ligature 6   - curse poem   being cursed

Look how cold it looks on the yellow linoleum, she said.
Like watching a thumb war, he mumbled.
Spent the whole fucking morning with the dishwasher man, she alerted
  him.
Standing in line watching the nape of the man in front of me, he
  remembered.
Perseid meteors from the radiant in the predawn, she read.
Is it really called Sutra of Angular Severity, he wondered.
Crossed out and then stetted, she noted.
High-speed dust fluorescing as it collides with solar wind, he read.
Now it's flu season, she wondered, should we give the boy an eye-wash?
They call it painting your throat, he noted, dipping the gauze in iodine.
In their component fatigue, the days… she mumbled.
And then you were talking in a French patois and wanting to go out, he
  said.
To be defiled is to be unrecognizable to yourself, she thought.

The quotidian takes over and makes you forget who you are. When you realize your life has taken over who you are.
irregularities of syntax embodies the welling of everyday life.

C. S. Giscombe

Poetry and the Oblique

Realize that *oblique* is a kind of dissent from a straight line, from the party line, from a line you're supposed to toe. ("a. slanting; declining from the vertical or the horizontal. b. diverging from a straight line or course.")

I encountered the ghazal, the very old Indo-Persian form, in Jim Harrison's book *Outlyer and Ghazals* in the early 1970s and wrote and published some imitations of him back then. Nowadays, in these first moments of the 21st century, the form seems to be gaining popularity or at least getting some press. Case in point is that the late Agha Shahid Ali's anthology of "real ghazals," *Ravishing DisUnities*, came out in 2000, recently enough to be called current. The ghazals therein are "real" because they follow the traditional repetition schemes and Ali claims, in the introduction, that "the free verse ghazal in America . . . seems always a momentary exotic departure for a poet." Exoticism's real, a predictable if "invisible" result of liberal racism, maybe too easily shaped here into a cudgel. But the book's of interest to me because of the other claims made in that introduction— that linearity is not what's at stake, that ghazals are specifically about disunity, about things not holding together but diverging. Clearly said here and valuable for that. It's what I saw in ghazals a long time ago, what

This began as notes for the 2004 Modern Language Association panel, "Poetry and the Oblique: Three Poets," organized by Dorothy Wang. John Keene was the respondent. The two other poets were Will Alexander and Mark McMorris.

attracted me to them: the big consciousness of the disunity of the world, how stuff existed in oblique relation to other stuff.

That relation is also about the context beyond the form—where's the world or, better, what's the traffic situation vis-à-vis the poem? My formative automobile experience was my years (1971–73) in the employ of Capitol City Taxi in Albany, New York. The city's eight biggest streets extended like an obvious if overgrown hand up the hill from the Hudson, the splayed, too-numerous fingers all heading west: they jutted off from one another—or came together or apart—at angles peculiar to local circumstance. Black people lived downtown, on the south side (as in so many cities). I was from elsewhere, I was there for university, but took jobs in town—first at a liquor store, then with the big public hospital, finally as a taxi driver; but I lived in the university neighborhoods, my experience of Albany was uptown and white until I worked at the hospital—the Albany Medical Center—and then for Capitol City, for whom I spent my nights "driving those colored people around on the south side." Harryette Mullen on "difficult" black writers: "Their unaccountable existence therefore strains the seams of critical narratives necessary to make them . . . comprehensible, and thus teachable and marketable." My relation to the city was my entry into situations unpredicted by my circumstances; "unanticipated," said Harryette Mullen. I got my hair cut—always an issue—on the south side and there was a barbecue place where I would eat sometimes too way down on Broad Street or Seymour Avenue, my big orange Checker perched outside. The only black driver (for the first two years), often the one black kid in the seminar. Human facts—your hair growing out like that, the need to eat and how food tastes. Sometimes you get sick and there's no rhyme or reason to it; or you have to go across town and sometimes that's too far to walk. So many poor folks—black or white—didn't have cars then in Albany, in the 1970s, but the city was a jumble of cars, and often—at the places where those big streets split or came together—all the cars had the green light, true story, no lie.

This is 2005. I'm writing about the Midwest—there, that place—and about forms of public transportation. The region's called the fly-over states by folks on the coasts; likewise are ground-transit systems (the centerless railroad system and the spin on call-and-response that taxicabs provide) beneath much current notice. Art's the contrivance, there to have effect.

On the dais at the MLA we (the "Poetry and the Oblique" panel) were all five of color. The "audience"—overwhelmingly white. I'm a doctor's son but I never saw or heard of a black doctor in the year I worked at Albany Med. Still, there are many ways to meet and serve and tangle with the public, ways to talk in public that involve the "facts" of public speech. I haven't written ghazals in years. I don't think there's an important difference between poetry and prose.

(all time)

        What it is running over
into the attitude the taking place in

an economy of catch
as catch can the intersection

with anyone speaking in place
in landscape

with myself

w/ big metaphors rolling in from what it must look like
from outside:

I loved principle to know how to look walking
exactly away from it

my own heart voice over
negotiated distance

the score (the call & unbeautiful response
in together from well over the wavery godhead

        —to be music catching noisily at itself

repetition & casual unfolding

slow stealthy returns

(Blue Hole)

A hold the eye had on *in* (the whole, widening

a hold the eye has crossing & re

-crossing the same stream, crossing water in a wide

wave of heat past innocence/ way past

(the rest of color in *widest* ambiguities,

rhetorically understated:/ the past's *whole* self giving up,

giving up a particular, say,

a name vernacular & local (if temporary, if descriptive or *tho'*

(the nomenclature can't keep up w/ the descriptive *sequenced*

into place, a long stare into the difference in place

of ceremony (of unexaggeration

a painted syntax way past the heart place of wch (being faceless

& not a source but wide

nor to the source but repeating undeceptive surface,

not source's s'posed-to-be (or love's

(repeated

(almost visible

(Hand-eye coordination)

      With sound

and the will

                 to trace
        back along it

                        (as though
                sound were a map of the city,
        skeletal, just
                        the big streets/ piano music
                for one hand)

            to what-
        ever is all
                & exactly the heart

            from which
        could come/ did come

                        this trouble,

                    the difficulty
        which is not in movement
        around or within

                        but through the fact of living
                somewhere
        in time,

                the point being
        to have
                (not "create")
        effect:

                hand   eye
                                (or
                    the mind's eye
                        anyway),

        grace
                & the physical complications
                inherent,

                    that is,
the real raggedness
                    of forward,

            of out
                    (at large)
        into the parks
                    & neighborhoods.

*

            Red as sin
comes the sun
                    up over moneyed DeWitt:

low hills, low
(ranch-style)
            houses,

        the eastern range
of the city & its suburbs

                        toward a lessening
of intensity & noise
                    more than some point
            things could reach & end at,

as speech does
            or the *will* to speak

& in a dream
            of the silence Just
After The Revolution,
                    I manage effect
            at some distance,

        standing up
through the sunroof of my Saab,

                        (K driving, slowly)

shooting out
every stoplight on Erie Boulevard

from downtown
the entire way

(the road divided
& continuous, both,

& bending slightly
without color
into DeWitt.

*

Into the sound
of dogs
barking behind fences, each
at the end
of his own chain,

not just here
but all across town,
almost a constellation,

an arrangement
we could discern,

deftly point to

& call the heart
of this savage time beating,

as though that would be
enough
& final,

and not consider
that the wild dogs too,
the coyotes,

have entered the city,

not howling
(as we, under
estimating,
would have expected)
& so beyond our account

except in the vaguest
& most single detail, never enough
even for the clutter

which poses as *narrative*,

A to B
to Z,

& inbetween
the similarity
of noise
over distance.

(The canal)

The narrowness
in places
of standing water,

all that's left
& older boys swim there,
their legs
dangle
from the locks.

K keeps 2 ferrets
in a pen on the back porch
(one fitch-colored,
the other white)
but rain drives their stench

indoors
   & the smells of overflow,
        of dead fish
    & leaves.

The TV forecasts more;

National Geographic comes, takes
       slowshutter pictures
     in color
of the Boulevard *a nuit,*
      single streams
     of tail-
    & headlights
      zigzagging to one side
for the flooded sections,
      low-
lying areas warns the TV,
      a swamp first
     & always.

      In a dream
    the ferrets swim
across the canal, back
     & forth,
back & forth between the high sides
like slow music

    & I remember the reflection
of my own body,
     diving,
    as though it were stopped there
         (not out over this
       dead water,
       but a wide spot
     in the river near home)

the second before
I closed my eyes;

it was not me
they saw in trouble from the shore,
the old tow-path,

         & later the police said

     it was nothing at all but carp
active at the surface
& mistaken

      for the clutching hands.

Far

Inland suffers its foxes: full-moon fox, far-flung fox—flung him yonder!
went the story—or some fox worn like a weasel round the neck. Foxes
are a simple fact, widespread and local and observable—Vulpes fulva,
the common predator, varying in actual color from red to black to rust
to tawny brown, pale only in the headlights.

It's that this far inland the appearance of a fox is more reference than
metaphor. Or the appearance is a demonstration. Sudden appearance,
big like an impulse; or the watcher gains a gradual awareness—in the
field, taking shape and, finally, familiar. The line of sight's fairly clear
leaving imagination little to supply. It's a fact to remember, though,
seeing the fox and where or, at night, hearing foxes (and where). The fox
appearing, coming into view, as if to meet the speaker.

Push comes to shove. Mistah Fox arriving avec luggage, sans luggage.

Favorite Haunt

Having lost the talent for driving and become, simply, "unavoidable," I
got to be an appearance at the center of things, a common apparition,
neither heaven nor hell.

No consequences, but the continent itself: this is writing from
experience, this is certainty past arrival, the flat center having become

my favorite haunt. I got to be an image, an appearance in the literature. (It means the same thing really, being allowed to *make* appearances and over a long time *becoming* a fixture in the imagination of someplace, famous there in a manner of speaking.)

Appearance to whom?

Staying on around the place, continental, a neighborhood man, a favorite ha'nt (or a favored one), fixed, Lincoln-esque, a little happy. Simple, but lots of folks are simple.

The open set, the open return.

Prairie Style

The direction giving out—in the business past direction then and avoiding love's blunt teeth there. Done with houses and wanting to be seen as a boundary or as a line of plot re-appearing, done with all that too. Houses cleave and, to me, it all gets hammered out in overstatement—love's a terror, a revelation cleaving to contours. Love's a terror, in town and out of town too.

I was an unqualified marker, some days the ache of an implicit region. Nothing to the bear but the curl of the self. Having missed the trace the first time through I found coming a specificity hard to pronounce: river of unaccented speech, a single voice to mark it all off. Well this is namelessness up here, this is inward, this is the equivocation of location and nothing but the curl will do.

Love's over there, to me, the old terror.

Nature Boy

Air over the place partially occupied by crows going places every evening; the extent unseen from sidewalk or porch but obvious, because of the noise, even from a distance. Noise glosses—harsh, shrill, a wild card. Sundown's a place for the eye, crows alongside that. Talk's a rough

ride, to me, what with the temptation to out-talk. At best long term
memory's the same cranky argument—changeless, not a tête-a-tête—
over distance: to me, the category *animals* excludes birds, the plain-jane
ones and birds of passage, both. To me, song's even more ambiguous—
chant itself, the place of connection and association. It's birdless, bereft.
I'm impartial, anhedonic. I'm lucky about distance but I would be
remiss if I didn't hesitate over image before going on.

Peter Gizzi

As I listen to a poem unfold in my ear it becomes clear that for every line I hear there are more lines resonating in the same field of meaning. Listening is everything in poetry: to the silences, the pauses, shifts in syntax, tone and content. Always for me a poem is about tracking what is not said and the particular place I can go to know what that is by what is stated. As if there are always two poems in my ear. What amazes me is how specific the "other" or phantom poem can be, and it occurs to me how language, when arranged, manipulated, built, or what you will, is saying both readings—together and separate. I imagine that the lyric is next to my life, but it isn't my life at the same time that it is real. Think of breath on a mirror. Sometimes, if I'm lucky, I can record this "other" poem and make it my own. But mostly it is a fragment felt and struggled with. I find myself left to develop the ruins of what did not come through. These hours spent listening, however, are what I believe to be the exceptional experience of poetry.

I guess what I'm after is closer to an environment, an experience of structure that collects in me. This condition of openness also figures a constant grappling with absence and lack. In a sense all my work is about this reckoning and displacement, enacted through an experience of lyric possession. A form of animism, but in it I would replace essentialism or soul with aesthetics or an empty core, a kind of holding open to allow tendencies of cadence, form, tone, coloring to move through the space of writing: a force that is both a construction of self and an emptying of self—not autobiographical but autographical—flexible enough to accommodate figures, things, voices, documentation; to combine, build and dissolve being, boundaries—to somehow let the poem become itself.

Periplum

Put your map right with the world

The person who knows where
has made an accurate study

of here

As to know
implies a different reading

Somewhere

faith enters
and must be pinned and sighted

A church tower is good for reference
but losing ground

Still

satellites orbiting the earth
track a true arc

but perhaps too grand
for everyday distances

And never mind about the bewilderment

"I'm at sea"

Nocturne

The day is an abandoned article.
In this miscellany I cannot
find a way to speak.
To say water lights at eventide
is seamless. Indecipherable
cause that extends out
the window to steeple
leads to lip stain.
Having been in your mouth
I walk the finger of the sundial
home and bruise the winter skyline
to psalm. The day goes to ground
as the sun drags over antique hills
with only a memory of heat burning
in another quadrant of the brain.
And as for beauty—don't say it.
The day is down and I dismount.

Speck

Single the sky, pulled taut above earth
single the sky, above water. Bound
to bark and leaves. You are solo.

Blended into paint and forced into color
the song of a man in his bed at dusk
the sparrows lighting outside his window.

Lonely Tylenol

There I could never be a boy
—Frank O'Hara

You have to begin somewhere.
The devil of your empty pocket moves as escargot
up the artery of a hollow arm,
ending on the lip of your dismay—it shows—
in the Brillo morning of a shaving mirror.
It is that morning always, and it is that morning
now, and now you must fight, not with fists
but with an eraser. The duelist awaits a ham sandwich
on the dock where your ship comes in.
Be warned and without ceremony take your place
as you have before. Only look once
at the idiot chagrin and smile as you ready your slingshot.
You are not alone in your palindrome.
Why is it so hard to know everything it said
when the mirror spoke. The book is darker
than night. Do you read me?
This is written somewhere and no one can
read it. It is not for them but to you
it is a reproof from years of neglect.
There there. No place like home.

The Truth & Life of Pronouns

The truth and life of pronouns falls to the next in line.
Mirage shimmers continue into oceans, oceans maintain
a shimmer of mirage, a vertical cycle evaporates to fiction.
Ready access. A handy plot. Once there,
some are simply to "die out" in specific forms?
Then desert at twilight, a silence, the syntax loosely worn,
unremarkable bits revealing less than say proof of, "ah-ha," and "OK."
You are pleased with ordinary fictions, objects disappearing

without a mark. The transparent depth. A looking glass.
It wasn't a truth outside truth, and beyond it,
the inner truth stood up, a square frame of night
etched into eyelids. A face is embodied
when the face is a fiction. Say dead, say dead, say very dead.
Who will miss it? You were indifferent to dusk and its originality,
a hard copy, plain in commonality, a single person
xeroxed to the distant field. The foundation
of the pediment, now crumbled, has fallen and the distance
of this life has been a life. Say live, say live, say verily live.
Accepting the subtle and thorough failure that is becoming a clearing,
a ballroom where people are too distracted to listen, the solo
not gaining in volume evolves by sheer duration.
Any henceforth will be met from this.
A sentence written to express the awkward silence,
a letter drafted to occupy a landscape. The lecture canceled.
    The check bounced.
With luck we won't recover in that future time
and finally be free from the inability to love.
It is important there be no consolation in these words,
just as there is no consolation sitting alone on a holiday.
Innocent people complicating the plot twist into another tableau,
and unaffected, because it already hurts. And those aspects
would only lessen the blow which is pure and fitting.
A vapor trail lines out on the horizon,
not even the geese know its destination. To take our cues
from the bird's flight leaving only this shadow on water,
shadow of a face I wants only to recall. Memory
stagnates like frost and weeds in winter, and older, pain dulls,
unlike the fable that will tell of the lost beloved, there is nothing
that will lead to that name. That face. That noun.

A History of the Lyric

> And this is no other
> Place than where I am
> —W. S. Graham

1. Objects in mirror are closer than they appear

they are right next to you
in the lanes, hugging a shoulder

*

they twitter in rafters
calling down to your mess

in rays, crescents

the white curled backs
of snapshots tucked in a frame

eyes of the dead

*

there is a gimbal lamp, ledger
a table of solid deal

clocks & militaria

a dirty blotter
its crusty bottle, a plume

*

there are beetles and boojum
specimen jars decorated

with walkingsticks, water striders
and luna moths

a treatise on rotating spheres

*

this swivel chair, worn
from some years past

a few doubloons, powder horn
musket bag and tricorne hat

a cannon, its yawning round

*

they are closer than comfort
closer than night breaking

over the mountain face

empurpled, its silhouette
ragged, silver

unquantifiable in pixie dusk

*

closer than power lines
casting shadows on brush

breath, heart ticking
the prepared delay

as twilight settles
in waves and crests

a water fowl, hooded owl

*

an avant-garde
a backward glance

2. *The ethics of dust*

to think I have written this poem before
to think to say the reason I came here
sound of yard bird, clinking lightbulb

to think the world has lasted this long

what were we hoping to say:
ailanthus, rosebud, gable
saturnalia, moonglow, remember

I am on the other side now
have crossed the river, have
through much difficulty
come to you from a dormer closet
head full of dark
my voice in what you say

at this moment you say
wind through stone, through teeth
through falling sheets, flapping geese

every thing is poetry here

a vast blank fronting the eyes
more sparkling than sun on brick
October's crossing-guard orange

3. *In the garden*

Lateness is a dark and luminous thing
so true of early twilight.

I have known the morning to be darkest
upon waking. The pictures go away

and one is back to the thing of living.
Things to handle and attend:

Hawthorne, willow spear.

*

If the dark speaks what does it say
in a dark time. As words choose me

are they mine, and the counterpointing wind.
If a catalog inserted here, your name here.

If the road turned, if your erratum
came to naught (for *with* read wick,

for *tear* read torn), if you found me.

*

This night dissolves outlines—trees,
leaves and power lines along the way.

What way? The goodly silence
returns its music as lateness falling

falls back into nerve.

*

So things come together, one
and one. And if one, and if

an overwhelming sense of rescue:
fallen leaf. Broken acorn. Schoolyard tears.

A grandiosity for being useful:
burning ship. Buckling dam.

*

Jets report a mass of shaped sound
off beyond the tree line.

I wanted to go to it: if leaf beauty,
if cloud beauty, if ideas of relation.

4. To his wife far off in a time of war

that you are not among the winter branches
the door opening
a trapezoid in deep gold light
I awoke to water in the distance
rushing loud as traffic on High St.
more real than traffic on High St.
if you were to come now
hair draping your shoulders
were to kiss my neck
bending to clip the flower
a happy lover might be
known to run to excess
but tell me am I happy

5. A history of the lyric

I lost you to the inky noise
just offscreen that calls us

and partly we got stuck there
waving, walking into the Percy grass.

A sinking pictorial velvet spray
imagining vermilion dusk.

You lost me to your petticoat
shimmering armor

saying it is better here
on my own amazon.

Why can't we or is it
won't you leave your solo ingle

beside the page. Did we never
consider life lyric interruption

to the idyll, laboring to rescue
real time, lost in affection.

Back roads dead-end in every epoch
but our view was singular, private

shared vistas of original walks.
Don't trade on this high tone

for silence, rather lumen chatter
recalling the better part of majesty.

6. Coda

When the sky came down
there was wind, water, red

When the sky fell
it became water, wind
a declaration in blue

When the end was near
I picked up for a moment, joy
came into my voice

Hurry up it sang
in skiffs and shafts
Selah in silvered tones

When the day broke open
I became myself
standing next to a door

In my dream you were alive
and crying

In Defense of Nothing

I guess these trailers lined up in the lot off the highway will do.
I guess that crooked eucalyptus tree also.
I guess this highway will have to do and the cars
    and the people in them on their way.
The present is always coming up to us, surrounding us.
It's hard to imagine atoms, hard to imagine
    hydrogen & oxygen binding, it'll have to do.
This sky with its macular clouds also
    and that electric tower to the left, one line broken free.

Bolshevescent

You stand far from the crowd, adjacent to power.
You consider the edge as well as the frame.
You consider beauty, depth of field, lighting
to understand the field, the crowd.
Late into the day, the atmosphere explodes
and revolution, well, revolution is everything.
You begin to see for the first time
everything is just like the last thing
only its opposite and only for a moment.
When a revolution completes its orbit
the objects return only different
for having stayed the same throughout.
To continue is not what you imagined.
But what you imagined was to change
and so you have and so has the crowd.

A Western Garden

The fog dictates lost sailors
tumbling in the waves.
We're almost home
the sine and cosine sing,
the clear single azure dome
and shiny air all say.

•

The wood grain is deeper
than a forest
deeper than the sea.
The solid indication
of space in time
these whorls testify
this pattern inside.

•

Whoa, Saturday.
Whoa, morning.
The wind chimes
empty the air,
sculpt the empty blue.

•

To be here in this light.
In this table lamp light.
In the overhead table lamp light.
To find oneself
on a quiet street
in a written speech.

•

So often we measure
by what is false.
We should measure
by what is barely legible
barely in our dailiness.
It is the invisible that doesn't lie

the invisible through which
we see ourselves finally
on a back street in the world.

•

The dark falls fast these afternoons.
The edge of sky moves in.
The sea and night are the same.
The fog and the night are the same.
The night is dark by the sea.
Can you hear the night?
Can you hear the chimes
the sea and the sky?

•

In a western garden
there are broken tiles
like the broken history
like the objects broke under
the rims of the conqueror's wheels.
In a western garden
it gets darker faster.
It is home this dark
this flag invisible in wind.

•

Standing at nth and twilight,
at twilight and liberty
ordinary as molecules.
The sun moves along the horizon.
Pedestrians float
across the esplanade.

•

The form of fire is air.
The form of water is air.
The form of air, earth.
Moving. Breathing. Burning.

Brenda Hillman

Seam Poetics

<>Who-Who x 3. A great horned owl in the pine outside. *Bubo virginianus.*<>In his visionary epic *Milton,* Blake invents a character called Shadowy Female who has trouble with space. The poet's psyche & society might redeem her.<>I was born the year they put power steering in Chryslers. Several things prepared me for poetry: "nature," "music," & "invisible layers." My landscapes were the Arizona desert, Mississippi (father), & Rio de Janeiro, Brazil (mother.) Desert, forests, cities all seemed inhabited by spirits; each shape had a lining of spinning energy. *Estou com saudades*—my mother's phrase—I am homesick/full of love. My family religion, an inward Baptist variety, affirmed that even inhuman things have Thought as a feature. The invisible agreed: Jesus lived in a cactus.<>My breath was taken away by poetry. How could such memorable forms Exist? Maybe children are drawn to poetry because the disequilibrium between themselves & reality is greatest then. First Millay, Keats, Dickinson & Ecclesiastes. I read Levertov's *O Taste & See,* wrote to her through her editor: How can a little girl become a poet? She wrote back, "Do not do what other people tell you to do in your poems."<>Poetry meets us. Adolescence is a great time to read Modernist poets, especially Eliot & Stevens. I heard a famous poet say: "The High Modernists ruined poetry for us." Why do people trash the Modernists? Modernism re-invented consciousness, re-imagined fragmented existence in cities, included alienated mind & nature, accommodated processes of uncertainty. Made God

flail, as well he should have, after WWI.<>My brother Brent gave me Plath in high school. Listened to *Blonde on Blonde,* the greatest album of all time.<>In college: Romantic poets with their distress, Symbolist poets with their moody atmospheres, Mayakovsky's "clouds in trousers," eucalyptus trees with their smog, Los Angeles Vietnam war protests, California freeways, nice drugs. Handed Luke Menand many surrealist poems; they were skinny as dorm beds. Collective dream nature. Jacques Maritain writes "The more the poet grows, the deeper the level of creative intuition descends into his soul." Listened to *Blue,* the greatest album of all time.<>In the early seventies at Iowa the poetic ideal was what was called "clarity." But the ideal poems seemed quite complex in that regard. Three of my favorite books were John Ashbery's *Some Trees,* Robert Hass's *Field Guide* & John Wieners' *Nerves.* Studied Charles Wright, Robert Duncan. Drank. Laughed. Ran around.<>Moved to Berkeley the year Saigon fell. Chris Evert was winning in tennis. My goal: to write for women who were struggling. I heard a famous poet say: "Women poets don't have world views." We were inventing many feminist poetries in the seventies, the first whole generation to try to write, have jobs & families. My friend Patricia Dienstfrey & I talked about poetic form. If you go down deep enough into the psyche, it is multiple. This could be shown in odd sentences.<>Recently a young poet asked me: "What was at stake for you as a poet in the eighties?" Place the best word you can find next to another; add space. That's my poetics. What was at stake was going to work, taking care of family. Experience was literary but not theoretical. The absolute horror of Reagan's good cheer: Oliver North saluting + Garfield the Cat stuck to car windows. Owls became endangered. Poetry had to include more forms, nuances, half-feelings, politics. I believe in one goddess, Mother All-Flighty, Mixture of heaven & earth. Young poet: avoid traps of convention. Write as big mind not as little ego. Collaborate but don't conform.<>Through several decades, struggling with inherited depression, I worked with trance & self-hypnosis. These irrational forms of knowledge are close to the sacred, as are numbers. Punk rock, Gnosticism, feminist theory, bird manuals informed my writing practice. Bob is my copilot. Alchemy, sex, cooking. Loosen the margins of the poem; give up on identity.<>Some think that, in order to retrieve a "general" readership, poetry should be easier to understand. I think not. Poetry needs to include the fragmentary, the uncanny, & the baffled. I've always feared programmatic aesthetics—even of experimental writing. Some poets reject emotion in poems—as unmediated romanticism. I prefer Barbara

Guest's remark: "All poetry is autobiographical."<>Poetics as praxis vs. ideal. To present multiple & oblique views of human conditions: wild styles, magical compositions, compressed thought. Innovation that embodies unofficial, profound experience. The lyric experimental tradition has been long & inclusive: The Shulamite, Herbert, Vallejo, Celan.<>I wrote *Cascadia* to bring together a tradition of radical nature writing— Gary Snyder—with feminist spiritual practice; Romantic, Symbolist, Modernist & Post-modernist experiments might cohabit the page. I knew the odd look might not be easily received as "nature writing." But that is what I was going to do.<>Some of our present tasks as poets: to protest the invasion of countries, the greed of multinational corporations, & the elimination of species under the rubric of Protection. To address inventively the poverty of the imagination in our culture. Walter Benjamin's *Arcades* shows history as a constellation, repeating and changing. Of course, activist poetics is/are more than writing poems. Jackson Mac Low, may Gertrude rest his soul, said a few years ago: "I am an anarchist; for years I didn't vote, but this time I'm voting." Americans need their poets to present difficult truths in subtle ways.<> "What kind of poetry do you write?" a stranger sometimes asks. I answer something to the effect that I write an alternative kind of nature poetry. Long pause. The person usually says, I don't read much poetry. I want to say: *Remember when you read poetry as a little child? You have unfathomable perceptions in the world. Poetry did not abandon you.*<>The spiritual life of a poet is dialectical, full of unresolved struggle that is simultaneously terrifying & pleasurable. I hope some of my words will speak to, and of, a specific & collective spirit of my age.

Thicket Group

> *... a burning liquid that was called the original force of Nature*
> —anonymous tenth-century alchemist

A POWER

For some reason it's likely to think of the insides of a thicket
    as a five-pointed liquid star.

A group of us, not knowing how to stand in nature, in the
    sixties; each breath sponsored by that.

Possible friends nearby smelled like hemp, white tortillas

and twelve-oz. Coca Colas; the fire in their fingers
talked back, had feelings.

Locating consciousness, where would you say it is;
    "it was the happiest moment in the first twenty years."

And, why do we seek to destroy it by changing?

                                        mottled doves

                                        garnets

———————————

EMPTY SPINES

Magic fought with the ideal, time
    curved the barren glow, and animals called from their
    nests at the center of the world.

I had been a child being guessed at by onyx, fresh
    from nothing. Dimension's pawn.

My brother okayed the ground with sticks; when
    something called, we answered it. With a drop or two
    more of that inherited chemical we would have been
    a schizophrenic.

Empty spines of sticks filled up with liquid fire; they had done this
    before, we just hadn't been quiet enough to mention it.

Making theories of creation is about repetition, though even
    the infinite happens just once.

                                        XX sticks
                                        cross-referencing
                                        each other

A WINDOW

Had intended to climb out a window, but intended is not
   what makes it happen. Delicious to climb out a window.
   The weather was not the window's fault.

Smears on chrome fenders like pet clouds between which
   they might see a body coming curved to them. Before
   the thicket your mouth stopped off at a boy.

Going back a little: nearing them was faster; that which
   owned the thicket also owned the flower.

Either tell the story or don't. Narrative is such an either/or
   situation, like a window, just as sex is a metaphor for
   not getting it.

You have changed the assignment to Swirl: voice from
   a thicket; surfaces meet where you live into things.
   A body is a place missed specifically. They met you
   in your body, where you couldn't go alone.

                              The spell:
                                   unable
                                   unable
                                   unable
                                   pretty soon

THE THICKET

A power came up; it was in between the voices.
   It said you could stop making sense.

Have you seen it? Of course you have. Based on
   what? A red bird that caught on fire on the alchemist's
   table.

The girls stood around in long paisley dresses, coyote cries
    coming through them, something frightened and
    being canceled. We weren't on drugs then.
    The thicket looked like a star of pub(l)ic hair.

You always want to control how everything will turn out,
    is the problem.

Suburban kids—on the edge of change—give up hope of being
    understood. Why did the fire need to rest in us after
    that fluttery little absolute terror of childhood.

                            (wands being

                                on fire)

DUST DEVILS

A power came up. It flew toward the guessing Cloud.
    It was not as curved as night or straight as day.

Have you heard it? Of course you have. It settled in the
    lyndon-johnson desert, supervising funnels,
    Eisenhower-bird-egg-head, stomach of peace and battles.

Standing before the thicket in long clothes not having sex. In the
    bible, you can't worship fire without worshipping dust,
    and whether you fought depression had everything to do
    with this.

A fire undaunted by the place where the years live.

To be patient with the kind of plot in which nothing happens,
    alchemists devised a burning water that didn't wet
    the hands. Elements mixed, swirled together, became
    decorative. Art comes from loneliness.

Air for Mercury

1.

After the double party
for the poorly loved

when the gleam in the hound's eye
fell like glass rain on the south

lawn of the countergarden, when
the image of false flags sank

in the mirrored plaques,
when the mirrored plaques

had been passed in, they took
your days and gave them back,

before you unsnapped first
the crenellated shoulder wings

then the fumbling then the little
ankle wings and sent them back

to the wing patrol, in the box,

in the metal box, in the genital
mouth of the rose (the open forms

of the state left so
undone that you were stranded

on the nonimperial coast having
a boat unnamed for you)

you were free, you were
having a bout of meaning—

II.

A leaf hurried by on its
side. Of what is knowledge made?

A season stopped by without your
noticing, saying, lost file, breath boy;

the sun had leaked its power
into things, and all notation had

become inaccurate suddenly, you'd been trying
to talk to them from this

coast, you'd been trying to help
them in their small groups.

III.

Monsters of will and monsters of
will-lessness confront the garden; a dragon

crow greets the dusk with its
prow. Rhyming is a tool of

friendly desperation. The spirits will return
though they're not here now.

IV.

Oracles, iron, the misuse of fire
under the young earth, and this

business of being infinitely swept up
in possibility so when you put

your hand down on something white
you noticed that detail, punctuated by

luckless forms. But night had been
deployed: see-through parts of the moon:

lace, *anima mundi*; and weren't there
two forevers, words and space, between

which more *experience* might ride, unencumbered?
You were supposed to tell them

what they'd missed; they'd read your
logics, your letters. So little space

between your letters, the words couldn't
easily air themselves. Remember going back

and forth between the rooms? Blue,
green; the wings had been adjusted.

You were meant to take black
netting off a face or two. Take

something. Passion brought you
here; passion will save you.

Air in the Epic

On the under-mothered world in crisis,
the omens agree. A *Come here*   follows for reader & hero through
the named winds as spirits are
lifted through ragged colorful o's on   butterflies called fritillaries, tortoise shells &
blues till their vacation settles under
the vein of an aspen leaf   like a compass needle stopped in
an avalanche. The students are moving.
You look outside the classroom where   construction find little Troys. Dust
rises: part pagan, part looping. Try
to describe the world, you tell   them—but what is a description?
For centuries people carried the epic
inside themselves. (Past the old weather   stripping, a breeze is making some
6th-vowel sounds *yyyyy* that will side
with you on the subject of syntax   as into the word *wind* they
go. A flicker passes: air
let out of a Corvette tire.)   Side stories leaked into the epic,

told by its lover, the world.
The line structure changed. Voices grew   to the right of all that.
The epic is carried into school
then to scooped-out chairs. Scratchy holes in acoustic tiles pull the whwhoo -- from
paperbacks. There's a type of thought
between trance & logic where teachers   rest & the mistake you make
when you're tired is not breathing.
The class is shuffling, something an   island drink might cure or a
citrus goddess. They were mostly raised
in tanklike SUVs called Caravan or   Quest; winds rarely visited them. Their
president says global warming doesn't exist.
Some winds seem warmer here. Seme.   Warriors are extra light, perhaps from
ponies galloping across the plains.
Iphigenia waits for winds to start.
Winds stowed in goatskins were meant   to be released by wise men:
gusts & siroccos, chinooks, hamsins, whooshes,
blisses, katabatics, Santa Anas, & foehns. Egyptian birds were thought to be
impregnated by winds. The Chinese god
of wind has a red-&-blue cap   like a Red Sox fan. Students
dislike even thinking about Agamemnon. You
love the human species when you   see them, even when they load
their backpacks early & check the
tiny screens embedded in their phones.   A ponytail holder switches with light,
beguiled. Iphigenia waits for the good.
Calchas & her father have mistaken the   forms of air: Zephyr, Boreas, Eurus
the grouchy east breeze & Notos
bringer of rains. Maybe she can   see bones in the butterfly wings
before they invent the X-ray. Her
father could have removed the sails   & rowed to Troy. Nothing makes
sense in war, you say. Throw
away the hunger & the war's   all gone. There's a section between
the between of joy & terror
where the sailors know they shouldn't open the sack of winds. It
gives the gods more credit. An
oracle is just another nature. There's   a space between the two beeps
of the dump truck where the
voice can rest. Their vowels join   the names of winds in white
acoustic tiles. A rabbit flies across
the field with Zephyr right behind.   Wind comes when warm air descends.
The imagined comes from the imagined.

Enchanted Twig

Sunlight tosses the small grasses its brain method. Once
  it gave us
  a dynamic hurt but we've gotten
    over it. Wobbly jay: the aspen is see-thru today, waiting
   for the Ice Age, & alphabets appear in
   every stem of it, tail shaking to a Y
  not far from ecstasy.
       Diverted creek sounds sad & maybe we better take
our dowsing stick out to the field, for our Y will
pull and
find buried water. With twig lines on our face and humming. With up
 & down for the world needs
  a water-finding stick for bringing wrecked water
sideways
beneath blue mist—   For water wants to be equal. Water wants
   to be equal and the world
      needs women with sticks & dusk husks, since they have
     taken the husks
  of damselflies when they straightened
   the creek, when the golf course needed its tight white
    globals (though the cowbird's yellow beanie eye
will survive the terrible pocked ball)—
Where there is a break in the fence near sweet horses we will skip
through
& hold down our stick in a shiny chipping field, cabbage white
  butterflies in pairs, pennyroyal—   Diet Pepsi plastic on its side & to
        the diverted creek & old creek bed
        say Meet
    this dowsing wand Come in—
        Mist bits rose this morning as I
crossed the field; heard the crooked cries cry creek to me,
  cried creek to me unable that the world wants
  water girls to work with mice, chipping off the blossom part of
 bitterbrush to save for later. Forced to mark
them out shy. Thanks for letting us know, hydrogen-times-two; leave
 the periodic
table and come to the dowsing stick, oxygen;

come to the water table— we are taking this finding down to
    delphinium,
       angelica, mimulus, letting water go or we will go at night,
  among introduced grasses, under the moons called Duir or
    Harvest, Deer Paw the Earth & Gort,
our stick
will dip down
in a Y for
Yes
it's here. Aspen, don't quiver, there's root parties a plenty and we will be wicked
    with our wick in our turn —<   the stick will summon
meandering stream for penstemon dandelion hair face,
       even the fungus beetle; those. Those qualities below. We miss our
         mother. Dear mother, daughter,
pilot, poet, sister,
  student, teacher, waitress, worker, water girls and girlie men, don't do
    their war;
         take Y rods, angle rods, bobbers, pendulums & loops
for the stick is the witch with dew,
electrons and glaciers the stick does do;
    for you miss your mother too and you can take your broken
      Y stick past the field they trapped energy in, poor stream,
        in their system there, to pull
          your water table up for water to be equal like the warbler
      building many nests against the imposter egg, will use that twig
    to mend the place where they have cut California in two.
    One at a time the simple
drops will come, though Agricola warned not to use the enchanted twig
  but you must come, it has
gotten serious.
So in binding oxygen to thin wild hydrogen and so in the earth you can
  bring energy
        from your
      stick water signatures, earth's meridian roused from a source,
  we will squint our ears to the babble & make for them a wavelength
    over the old new field—

for CB

Partita for Sparrows

We bury the sparrows of Europe
with found instruments,
their breasts light as an ounce of tea
where we had seen them off the path,
their twin speeds of shyness and notched wings
near the pawnbroker's house by the canal,
in average neighborhoods of the resisters,
or in markets of princely delphinium and flax,
flying from awnings at unmarked rates
to fetch crumbs from our table half-spinning
back to clefs of grillwork on external stairs
we would descend much later;

in rainy neighborhoods of the resisters
where streets were taken one by one,
where consciousness is a stair or path,
we mark their domains with notched sticks
of hickory or chestnut or ash,
because our cities of princely pallor
should not have unmarked graves.
Lyric work, flight of arch, death bridge
to which patterned being is parallel:
they came as if from the margins
of a painting, their average hearts half-spinning
our little hourglass up on the screen.

Claudia Keelan

The Present in Wilderness

In "Composition as Explanation" Gertrude Stein explains that what is being made depends on what everyone is looking at. She's speaking directly of World War I and trench warfare, of cubism, of the modern period's love affair with poetic innovation derived from natural phenomena—her use of the continuous present, homage to real time.

She found company for this endeavor in Picasso and Matisse, in other painters and writers whose methods were derived from a desire to expand the available reality. In that sense, she and her friends were freed from the pursuit of "art" into the pursuit of Being.

It's possible to talk about this pursuit as one where product is inherently linked to its construction, i.e., to the process of the piece. It's possible to get stuck in that conversation, processing endlessly, the present under siege, fingers dirty in the materiality of it all. It's possible, at the other extreme, to opt out of the conversation altogether and remain continually interested in your own indecision, in your ultimate disinterest in real time—the only actual place poetry gets written—and perpetuate an empty lyric, innovative all right, interested in Being all right, but ultimately empty of anything but you, you, you.

There's nothing remotely interesting, true, or humorous, last and most important, about either possibility.

I'm writing this at the end—the beginning—of what started as Operation Enduring Freedom and evolved into Operation Iraqi Freedom.

For weeks everybody's been looking at a palimpsest of Baghdad. We're watching the predetermined conqueror forge a medieval path, a column of trucks and jeeps that drive as slowly as a crusader might have ridden, weighed down in armor. It's so funny I'm crying. The bombing of Baghdad happens in the dark. Based on a paradigm of conquest, the war we witness is successfully erasing the validity of the Other, and we are going backwards in time, the enduring projects of the great civil movements of the last century—in India, in America, in the individual life projects of many—which offered the action of the One for the Whole—invalidated.

> How easy to slip
> into the old mode, how hard to
> cling firmly to the advance. (W. C. Williams)

The Other is in you and is everywhere so her death too is yours, and yet there is no We / is only We. See how we are not going backwards in time; see how the royal we has reached a new/old barbarism. Invalidation is the point, validation, a process given official sanction. The aesthetics of Operation Enduring Freedom are backwards and some are thus liberated by the knowledge in the difficult present.

My's purposes remain the same. I wants to reach You. You may be lost in your he/she and merrily I's there too. What a company!

In the beginning *their* is war, in black and white, before dinner, each night, a jungle and helicopters and Selma and Birmingham and my brother and I run in the dark before sleeping. In the beginning words and books and in the books the words I loves   love thine enemy
    be kind to those who hurt

And yet I needs friends and where are they

Harold Bloom wrote a piece in 1998 for the *Boston Review* that sparked a forum in a subsequent issue. In his article he proposes that all great poetry is of the self; in it, he also laments multiculturalism and acting as a proponent for, as Reginald Shepherd so aptly avers, "an etiolated version of Romanticism," he makes the mistake of writing: "they have the numbers; we, the heights . . . " Marjorie Perloff wittily spars with "Remarks," as Gertrude Stein so nicely put it, "are not literature . . . " and goes on to summon Frank O'Hara's unforgettable "personism" as rebuke.

Donald Revell gently admonishes Bloom by citing passages from Bloom's exemplars—Shelley, Whitman and Crane—that achieve, he says, "ecstatic self-effacement," bringing them happily down from the sobriquets re: "the divine" and "the sacred" proffered by Professor Bloom. Ann Lauterbach's extensive listing of anthologies from the modern period to the present illustrates that it is in its continued proliferation, multicultural at its heart, and not in the militaristic (and redundant!) "The Best of the Best," that poetry's "heights" are more closely approached: "A rose, after all, is still only a rose, but it smells sweeter when there are three of them." If Susan Howe had been asked to respond, I imagine she would have brought her brilliant and ethical redactor's mind to bear, bringing forward a newer version of the 1990 "There Are Not Leaves Enough to Crown to Cover to Crown to Cover" where she states: "History is the record of winners. Documents were written by Masters . . . I write to break out into perfect primeval Consent. I wish I could tenderly lift from the dark side of history, voices that are anonymous, slighted—inarticulate." Alice Notley, another poet I have never met but on the page, would surely have been adding from across the Atlantic: "It's necessary to maintain a state of disobedience against . . . everything. One must remain somehow, though how, open to any subject or form, in principle, open to the possibility of liking, open to the possibility of using . . . But NO DOCTRINES! I tend to think reality is poetry . . . " I love the poignancy of the aside inside the assertion, her knowledge that openness is correct, "though how" to maintain it, becomes the problem. There's not enough time to bring in all those with whom I feel company in the present. Certainly Bloom's *The Anxiety of Influence* gave me the permission to write *The Secularist* and he was the first to anthologize my work, a work which risks being repetitive in its adherence to negative capability. "Without contraries there is no progress" and Blake too knew how lucky we and our poetry are for it. I have many friends, living and dead, some closer to the truth than others, those who I have known all my life and those never met—Jesus, Paul, Buddha, the writers of the *Bhagavad-Gita*, Diogenes, Ovid, Longinus, most of the troubadours and trobaritz, St. Francis, George Fox, Gerard Winnstanley, Ann Hutchinson, Thomas More, Queen Elizabeth the First, John Keats, Sarah Coleridge, the Shelley who wrote "In Defense of Poetry," the Coleridge who wrote "Dejection: An Ode," Tolstoy, Dostoevsky, Rousseau, Rimbaud, Whitman, and all my practitioner compatriots in the last century and the present—whose methods, life and work enthrone me in a present mediated on all of our behalf.

Refinery

Let the words fall, please just let them.
With all we've abandoned by now
chances are we could piece the fallen
city together by recall, assemble

The family members for a new portrait.
We could put the terror in reverse: how
the black chalk eases off the faces and the blood
returns from the salt water, filling

The scattered limbs that are assembling now,
back onto the bodies. How the boys, enamored,
amnesiac, stare down at their boots until

They board the ships and sail back the way
they came, the sands left unstained,
apologies forgotten in their throats.

If Not In The Field Then Where

   The first of October and still
the insects deliver prayers in an idiom not understood
but for the emphasis, can you hear it, on finish. All summer
their large republic, unholy choir, punctuated
the actions of things until it was impossible
   to live here without them. That music everywhere so that
even the littlest boys fumbled catches in the baseball field,
their parents' digressive, troubled love, *that's my boy*
seemed rote, orchestrated. And then the falling down
of days, deals in car lots, the order of the church bell,
   rubble, rubble. I tried to catch one today, cicada, good
word. I even had a glass jar. I walked the periphery of the
town, I stood on the edge of a far field. I entered the field.
I got down on my knees, I crawled, jar in my mouth. I peeled
the brown leaves of corn, looked for it in the fruit

If not in the field then where, and I'm stroking
the unseen, following their directive to its very edge: not in
the trees, but *in* them, not on the road, but by it. not in this
listening, but through it. Here? In the neighborhood's lie
of order, this promise among us? Here, teacher, in the headlights
    in this stumbling travel, I am afraid
of the intermittent flashing of light that I must touch the body
of this sound in, because fingering these silken wings might still
it, my head uncovered, unprepared in earnest
for this snow I fall in.

The Modern Life of the Soul

    This road through the middle of us,
this love like a civil war photograph where action
couldn't be developed so they were forced
to pose together, smiling. And then the solidarity
of the killing fields, all their limbs (count them)
    transcribing some kind of flight there. Twisted, (click).
Running, (click, click). Those fallen and empty uniforms,
an effigy the blue gray of this morning poses somehow,
chairs rocking alone on the front porch, the whole house
leaning towards the road single cars pass
    through every hour or so. Three dogs sniffing the edges
of the lawn, a wasp striking the screen a gunshot
down the road the dogs trotted. Is this where this will end
today? *Loyalty won't be coming home today, I'm sorry?*
That sound the period the day allots at the edge
    of the far field? And then the sorry aftermath,
calls pleading out across the corn regardless
of outcome, the *something* this road cut between neighbor's
land seemed to promise, left unretrieved for now. Somebody
made this road from what?—God's spoon? Carved it just perfectly
    really, right through the middle of possession, amnesiac for
a thrilling minute. This road through the middle
of us, this love, like a civil war photograph where action
couldn't be developed and how they were forced
to pose together, smiling.

And Its Discontents

The spirit is moving
the surface of the water
today, a school
of fish by light,
all mouth and forward
thrust, all mouth. What I can't see—
the body of a fish—and so
am drawn to light, blurring
the distinctions between in
-side and out, the mile
of surface light they wake,
lost now behind the trees.
Something mercenary promised.
The mouth of the withheld
open with laughter.
St. Anthony witnessing to the caught,
strung things, emptied of motion
there on the docks. Old voices,
old stories. Shoal,
shoal, mouthing
near the edge of a shallow.

But that was years ago.
What is retrieved, illusion,
God's finger a larger
form of water, manifest
most likely, in the tracings
the heart monitor or lie
detector would like to reveal. What is inside
spreading itself all over things,
the fishes, light-plagued, staccato
jumps, the beginning
of a machine's war,
or a version of rainbow.

                    Outside, debris,
week's end. The fish

too silver and other to be real
from the beginning. But the bird,
stunned by the window's half-truth,
flight passing from sight!
It stood and stared, not like *bird,*
but something shapeless, older and more
patient, for an hour until shadow
forced it back to name
then to motion then to—Neither instinct nor action!
A bird crooned is illusion,
is elsewhere, an effigy of time.

I live alone, have no neighbors,
though my love gathers crumbs
in the next room
and the old caretaker bleeds
our well, burns the old grass.
My body knows us,
withering into its truth, a statue
in a public garden.
In time, the catastrophes weren't enough.
The believers burn again
in the family hour, the hurricane
a form of fan,
the body a word collapsed
under a flag.
Writing was in its origin
the voice of an absent person.
In one hand, a basket of fish,
in the other, a ticket, or letter.
A little closer somehow.

While the Wind Speaks

All you have to do is try to keep it alive,
water in a manmade ditch with somewhere
to go. *Won't you get out of bed? Something*

out there needs you in it. All you have to do
is try to keep—But the succession of birds the cat
gets somehow by the neck—All we had to do was try to—
But the wild bled clean out of them, our misguided
hands washing the wound, putting on the salve.
It's not too deep, is it? It's not the wild
given up to will, is it? Because the wind blows through
the corn, right? Up and down each row and through
the corn, right? Until some days it's freedom itself
the corn won't allow. Until it's morning itself
we heard boxed in out there in the field. And the corn,
instrument of order, sorry when its won, laying down
its tassel flag, etc. etc. etc.

> Forgive me my day my teacher.
I'm listening, but the beagle keeps crying now
that hunting season is over. Neighbor of mine the dark won't
let rest, bred to sniff out the waiting. O.k. little brother,
I hear you. Over there. But it's only your master's clothes
strung on a line. Over there. But the chain link fence.
Inside the cage friend. Inside the cage, dig your pretty
face into the dirt.

Sun Going Down

The occasions wouldn't stop occasioning—

Occasion for happiness—
For stupidity with her feathered crown—
Occasion for dreaming—
Jack Spicer the best singer
In a salsa band
& the evil dwarf in mine
Looking for our bridal bed
In a room named after a towering plant . . .

Occasion for murder, daily,
The nation's transparent plans

Occasioning the bodies of the new soldier
Sportif in khaki and floppy hat,
Wide-spread Kentucky eyes too blue for horror.

Oh occasionally, occasionally—

Times for murder daily
At "home,"
Both army and Islam
Falling bus driver, shopping ladies,
School boy and all
Waiting at the occasional mall.
The occasion a sequence,
A symptom, a
Spate of minutes held
Momently in place by
Bodies, by action, by architecture;
By leaving the scene, not finding the room
Or finishing the song; by dropping your pants

& running freely in green-leaf-sand.

Occasion for nightmares not remembered.
For the radio all through the days,
For the missile shot from the Marshall Islands in the Pacific
To implode freely over our home in Las Vegas.
For my boy's terrible crying then,
And the life we shared together
Ending, I believed,
Until news came of the test—
This is just a test . . .
Is it all a test?
My mother thinks so,
Crooning beside the ashes of my father.

Occasion for hatred
For the men
At the Pistol Range,
For the flags smothering their trucks . . .

Occasion for dreaming
Of burning down the Pistol Range,
Of destroying the bulldozers
And cement trucks paving the Mojave;
Of gathering the flags and sewing them
Each to each into a shroud
For a country going down
In the aftermath light of its occasion.

Timothy Liu

A Multitude of Tongues

In my first book of poems, *Vox Angelica,* I implore the muse to "teach me how to sing in a grove of olive trees, / to fall as a sparrow" ("Ariel Singing"). In the last poem of my most recent book of poems, *Hard Evidence,* I remark that the "machine-gun fire of the underline key of a student's / Smith Corona [is] a *correspondence of words and action, / of name and actuality* while voices keep directing airstrikes / on Iraqi positions drowned by strong revanchist passions" ("Western Wars Mitigated by the Analects"). From first to last, these poems map out a lyrical terrain wherein that which is voiced or sung by the apprenticed self finds fulfillment in the illusory permanence and consequence of writing, war and love alike framed by passionate discourse. This movement from "singing" to "writing" parallels one's journey from "innocence" to "experience." It is a dance that abandons paradise but never ceases longing to somehow return to it, albeit unsullied by language. For me, such yearning is crucial, indeed at the core of composing lyric poetry.

As an aficionado of vocal performances from lieder to opera, I am aware that there are some marvelous singers who do not know how to read music, Pavarotti most famously. Here was a singer who was unable to *read* the written score and yet could somehow *hear* the music nonetheless, outsinging all others. Of course, he mastered his voice through rigorous training, but the notes seemed to have traveled directly from ear to throat, bypassing *text* altogether. Perhaps it is every poet's dream to be free of the poem, to simply pluck one's strings and sing as Sappho sung, the invisible text as transport rather than as fetish. Whenever a vocal performance is about to begin, I am torn between following the text/translation in the printed program (or subtitled screen) and simply closing my eyes to open my ears ever more to the actual presence of voice itself. If I know the words *by heart*, then all the better, but the words in and of themselves seem but handmaiden to the sacred voice that seeks to deliver us from profane time altogether.

But what is the garden if not a garden made of words? One hears the voice of God issuing forth commands in Genesis but one does not hear God sing. We may sing to the Lord, but the Lord does not sing back. If the Word was in the beginning, then perhaps the end shall be filled with singing: "And they sung a new song, saying, Thou art worthy to take the book, and to open the seals thereof: for thou wast slain, and hast redeemed us to God by the blood out of every kindred and tongue, and people, and nation" (Rev 5:9). When all the angels sing, it is in the Ur-tongue rather than in the multitude of confounded tongues that is the condition of our existence. American poetry is a Babel. "All art aspires to the condition of music." But who among us will sing the songs of love, death, and God? From the most extreme outposts of our islanded selves, we sing a dialect of one. And if indeed we are not slouching towards some apocalyptic rapture, then desire remains—that of not only *being heard* singing in and of our own times but perhaps in times to come.

In Flagrante Delicto

I. LETHE

sound asleep and shadowed by a crumbling pier the body of a stranger

caught in such autoerotic repose and if that rowboat drowned in sand

fails to budge or moonlit sails proclaim the absence of an actual wind

what marriage do we have that thrives on was instead of is to be a kite washed up on shore blackened shells strewn in trampled grass where

fires last night had been your kiss refused the taste of him ripped deep

inside the salt tide's aftermath inferno streaked eroding all remaining

sense of shore the dawn mere possibility where oarlock gently creaked

II. LIKE BOYS NEXT DOOR

channel surfing from baseball scores to late night news for images

of ourselves in vain no faggots here in uniform only shirts that say

repent or perish as closets open wide their flaming doors just try on

the face of a christ that took a lifetime of our suffering to achieve

last-pick sissies striking out foreheads marked with ash as tongues

begin to slide like eels in public parks tempting boys who'd flock

to sport some jockstraps stuffed down throats where teeth had been

knocked-out a pack of trading-cards some drag from base to base

III. JUST SOME BOYS

tossing frisbees in the eucalyptus scented air equidistant to the site

of old catastrophes waterlogged under a bridge our bodies pulled

to the center where it sags with years of connubial bliss and hardly an hour's peace on unpaved roads that lead to a drive-thru window

where shrooms were tucked in a happy meal why not spy on boys

who spread their legs under leaves so green you'd think it was a set

heaving in the heat forget that homeless voice that kept on shouting

how many easter eggs you want up your ass the two of us pushing

IV. ROMAN FEVER

gripped by a cell-phone panic day-trading shares a load more fun

than getting drunk on Jersey sky awash in amaretto light as I vespa

through the Palisades dependent more on Wall St. than the voice

of Pasolini now walling out all canyon echo clandestine rest-stop

action darting through the shrubs in search of Armani-suited cock

pack-muled through crevices at dusk patrol-car love winking past

that dogstar all aglitter over Ostia falling into the hands of rough

trade *che gelida mania* thread-bare boxers pulled down to our heels

V. HOME OF THE BRAVE

reduced to rubble our democratic vistas unable to outlast far-right

terrorists who plan to poison water supplies as we wine and dine in whistle stops trying to outbully operatic regicides curled inside

the tail of a treble clef floating on the outskirts of a forgotten town

where patriots bored from shooting at paper targets put complete

bomb-making guides online while orphans playing stick ball sift

through cases of crackerjack hit lists faxes anthrax sold by mail

some triggers and detonating fuses left inside that local ballot box

VI. HEAVY FREIGHT

a handprint fossilized on a child's startled face a bout of fisticuffs

as witness to love's excess straddling another bride as the bouquet

flies ferruginous tresses spilling over marble fonts into some abyss

eleemosynary grunts instead of sermons on the mount as grounds

for divorce where orphaned souls stampede down ungulated clefts

bikini wax ripped off depilatory forms to appease an ultramontane

satrap instructed in orthography by missionaries caught red-handed

in compromised positions trying to micturate into the rutilant night

VII. REQUIEM

a prayer pooling on our lips while semen spurts across the room into the laps of virgins hitched in stirrups all of 'em ready to ride

some heavenly horse out of life while candles drip into sockets

of candied skulls that crown a gravestone pulverized by lichen

in a field where couples lean against a crumbling wall the sound

of iron sandals drawing near Andrei Rublev on a board between

two ladders erecting icons in the dark even as Cocteau's woman

wanders onto a set with eyes painted on her eyelids that are closed

VIII. SIRENS SINGING

of a lover's eyes newly-minted in maternal din anxieties complete

with pink fiestaware jarring the hours a hundredfold where vocal

mutilations hover over a violin come unstrung no talk only grunts

washed up on shore all those hag-infested hours redolent with fog

her laughter's rickety bridge seldom crossed emotions clocking in

instead of punching out the taste of it percolating on that stovetop

licked by dawn by way of telegram a truce delivered yet somehow

always the wrong address the come-on instead of a goodnight kiss

Dau Al Set

Vocalise haunted still by faces smeared with ash.

Depressed all winter long he thwarts his captive breath.

If only we could plunder rumors kept well-guarded.

But are you there and are we troubling you?

The stars suffused with aspects no one can discern.

A maiden warming up to a widow who shields her face.

Who's to say our *ch'i* might not suddenly bloom.

Or rival a sage's flowering arms await the call.

The ceiling clay shouldered-in by solemn monks.

An oracle to be chosen where the bottle stood uncorked.

Lips without song useless as the hours pass.

Who asks for bread instead of stones flying overhead?

A sickness in the blood crowned with fire.

Renounce the troth or spare us six-winged seraphim.

Too much perhaps desired glazed with pearly glow.

As he forsook the root to try the bones again.

In mansions we cannot enter wider than this world.

Besieged by Roses Shot from Quivers

With alchemists gathering dew off leafy shrubs at dawn.

A sprig of rue hung above the cattle-shed door.

Where dried mullein dipped in fat had been lit up as a torch.

Before the brothel-heavy afternoon settled in.

Under that vaulted dome some called the castle of love.

Untold chivalric escapades soon espied.

Seated ladies sewing chaplets flanked by a turf bench.

By plasters applied to the abdomen to aid in their conception.

Lavender tied in bundles for chastity's preserve.

Blackouts to outlast five-hundred years.

Between the villa and the garden where scholars have failed.

Epithalamion

dawn's arrows poised for flight near banquet tables that run the entire
length of heaven

while radio signals from alabama disrupt a late quartet haunted by
squawks and jeers

that taunt us still all those frat boys wanting nothing but release their
tattooed anchors

sinking beneath black light where disco reigns triumphant with death
not far behind

our voices weak without the flesh without that white macaw and
cockatoo chanting rote

affections asking us to pay attention where lights go down on love letters
scrawled by

hand stacked shoulder-high to the wind as newlyweds now vanish
behind a storm of rice

Orpheus at the Threshold

The way she putzed around then dropped her panties to the floor.

The hourglass in her bedroom dependable as she.

In series was how the men arrived.

The openings of the body entered in a series not to be repeated.

A bathtub filled with roses browning at the edges.

A bloody sheet hung outside her hotel suite the only flag to be seen.

Descriptions of the act more memorable than the act itself.

What had been done on earth as it was in heaven.

The whole house petal-strewn.

And the weight of lava stone healing bloodshot eyes.

Nerve-rope armored in its case of bone awaiting a mother's touch.

Overcast

He says he feels more and more like the wife, meaning more
like furniture. An arrangement left on the coffee table to keep

appearances up. Perhaps we all can feel the silence she feels
smothered by—laughter's good weather suffused with bloom,

the streets but part of a siren song lovers walk without alarm.
Like gold that's sunk to the ocean floor—childhood's heavy

gold sinking even now as voices huddle outside the bedroom
door—our children as yet unkissed by dawn's advancing call.

Petty

violations teething throaty laughs as juveniles take a blowtorch to that
     stray some sissies

hypnotized by a casual bulge reciting verses that Rumi wrote in praise of
　　Shams buried

under mud that slid through windows nestled high on hills as footsteps
　　of past masters fit

stifling masks onto pressed hams spied through shower glass in that
　　parade of tongues

licking tender egos foisted onto thrones bejeweled with envy and regret
　　where fat trolls

watch jocks peel off their shorts on that private beach fenced-in by
　　porno stills unspooled

on the kitchen floor some hang-up calls the police can't trace as
　　hurricanes come and go

Nathaniel Mackey

Artist's Statement

I haven't been able to forget that the root of the word *lyric* is the lyre, the musical instrument the ancient Greeks accompanied songs and recitations with. It's not that I've wanted to forget, though at times I've wondered if it were something I'd made up or been lied to about, the lyric of late so widely equated with phanopoetic snapshot, bare-bones narrative, terse epiphany and such much more than with music. I also haven't been able to forget that for centuries poets in English have punned or played on *lyre*'s homophony with *liar*, suggesting an awareness of words' ability to mislead, a self-suspecting wariness we tend to arrogate to postmodernity. This I've in fact made an effort to forget, wanted to forget, wanting not always to be so wary as well as wanting not to remember that—contra one of our claims to originality even as we eschew originality—wariness and suspicion didn't just get here fifty or sixty years ago. Actually, I've wanted to and I've not wanted to.

Poetry, to echo Louis Zukofsky, is an art whose lower limit is check, upper limit enchantment. Or is it upper limit check, lower limit enchantment? Poetry is the art of having both—horizontally or, if not, each variably above and below the other. Our recent turn toward promoting check over enchantment wants to forget *lyric*'s etymology, as though the art might arrive at a point where there were no strings attached. But strings

are always attached, even in the most thoroughgoing doubt or disenchant-
ment. Even check, itself a sort of string, knows that.

    What to do then?

    Pluck, bow, strum, scrape, scratch . . .

["Waters . . . "]

    Waters
wet the
mouth. Salt
currents come
to where the
lips, thru
which the tongue
slips, part.

At the tongue's
tip the sting
of saltish
metal rocks
the wound. A
darkness there
    like tar,
like bits of
drift at ocean's
edge. A slow

retreat of
waters beaten
back upon
themselves.

    An undertow
of whir im-
mersed in
    words.

Song of the Andoumboulou: 55

—orphic fragment—

Carnival morning they
were Greeks in Brazil,
Africans in Greek
disguise. Said of herself
              she
  was born in a house in
heaven. He said he was
  born in the house next
door . . . They were in hell.
In Brazil they were
            lovebait.
  To abide by hearing was
    what love was . . . To
  love was to hear without
looking. Sound was the
             beloved's
  mummy cloth . . . All to say,
said the exegete, love in
  hell was a voice, to be spoken
to from behind, not be able
    to turn and look . . . It
  wasn't Greece where they
            were,
nor was it Benin . . . Carnival
morning in made-up hell, bodies
  bathed in loquat light, would-be
song's all the more would-be
  title, "Sound and Cerement,"
            voice

  wound in bandages
raveling
      lapse

•

Up all night, slept well
past noon. Awoke restless
  having dreamt she awoke on
    Lone Coast, wondering
  afterwards what it came

               to,
  glimpsed interstice,

                 crevice,
    crack . . . Saw her
dead mother and brother
pull up in a car, her brother
  at the wheel not having driven
  while alive, newly taught

             by
  death it appeared. A fancy car,

              bigger
than any her mother had had while
  alive, she too better off it
appeared . . . A wishful read, "it
  appeared" notwithstanding, the
  exegete impossibly benign. Dreamt

              a dream
  of dream's end, anxious, unannounced,
Eronel's nevermore namesake, Monk's
    anagrammatic Lenore . . . That the
  dead return in luxury cars made

             us
  weep, pathetic its tin elegance,

             pitiable,
    sweet read misread,
    would-be
    sweet

Song of the Andoumboulou: 60

The vote came in early. We ignored
     it. No ballot-box auction for us . . .
Nub's uninstructed dance's bare
          feet, music we took them for.
                              At a
     loss with only bodies to fend with,
          nonsonant waves kept coming,
sang without wind,   saltless,
     waterless,   Nub's inverted
run, Nub newly vented by horns
                              blown
     elsewhere, bells full of insect
          husks . . . Nonsonant scruff held
on to, sheerness . . . Nothingness
     it seemed we grabbed at, gathered,
beginning to be unending it seemed.
                              We
     were beginning to be lured again,
ready to be hectored, huthered, move
     on, beginning to be uprooted again . . .

     A peppered expanse the country we
crossed. Space doled out so stingily
          we wept, love's numb extremity
     the outskirts of Nuh, name whose
                              elision
     we embraced . . . A tale told many
times over, known before it reached
          us, known before we knew, un-
     backed alley of soul we wandered
                              into,
     shadowbox romance it was called . . .
Come of late to creation's outskirts,
rub's new muse a republic of none, a

yet-to-be band the band we were . . .
We were Andoumboulou, dreamt
                                    in-
    habitants of "mu," moored but
    immersed, real but made up, so much
        farther flung than we'd have thought . . .

They the would-be we lay on a bed
the size of Outlantish. Lip attesting
    lip, tongue rummaging tongue,
                                    took
    between finger and thumb the hem
of her dress, flat bead of sweat, salted
                                    cloth . . .
    A hammer hit them each on the head.
    Hammered heads rang and rang without
end . . .   Called it creation, called it
    their clime, close where there was otherwise
        distance,   mute endearment,   recondite
        embrace . . . So much farther, felt even
                                    so,
mouth she remembered, home. His to hear
    her tell it, hers were it his to say, whose
    book was of lengthening limbs, hers of
                                    the
unquenchable kiss . . . A tale told over and
                                    over,
    long since known by heart. Lay belly to
    back, turned belly to belly, each the other's
dreamt accompanist, music they made in
    their sleep . . . Frayed hem the interstice,
                                    time's
    moot rule. Time's moot rule amended,
                                    echoed
    advance it was
also called

A first unfallen church of what might've
been. Let run its course it would have
    gone otherwise, time's ulterior bequest . . .
This they had a way of imagining,
                this
    they so wished it to be. Abstract he
    at the back of her mind, she at the
back of his, each the other's Nub
    constituent, ghost of an alternative
                     life . . .
They were we before we were, ancestral,
                we
    who'd never not be ill at ease. A vocation
    for lack he'd have said, she'd have said
longing, a world, were they to speak, be-
tween . . . What wasn't, they'd have said,
                 went
    away, would come back, first fanatic
              church,
  what would
  be

  •

    They the would-be we talking talk of
election, devotees of Iemanjá. Glass-
    green water they were in up to
               their
    shoulders, each the other's moored
recess . . . The way she said his name stayed
with him. More made of what wasn't
    there than what was, whispered,
             came
back again . . . Love called out from side-

walk to balcony, rooftop to galaxy,
                              mute . . .
   More made of what was there than
      was there, mouths vow-heavy at
   bed's edge, lip-touch never to be done.
Never to get up again it seemed, lay
                              shaken,
      endlessly commemorative advent,
                              dreamt
      evanescent caress . . . A first unfallen
         church it might have been. Let
   run its course it would have gone
      otherwise, time's ulterior bequest . . .
This they had a way of imagining,
                              this
      they so wished it to be. Abstract he
         at the back of her mind, she at the
   back of his, each the other's Nub
         constituent, ghost of an alternative
                              life . . .
   They were we before we were, ancestral,
                              we
      who'd never not be ill at ease. A vocation
      for lack he'd have said, she'd have said
longing, a world, were they to speak, be-
   tween . . . What wasn't, we'd have said,
                              went
      away, would come back, first afflicted
                              church,
      what would be . . . We were caught in a
   dream whispering names we'd forget
      waking up, caught waking up or in a
dream of waking up, moot sound riffling
         our lips. Nub was a name,   was
                              was
      a name,   a was a name, all moving

on . . . Names came after us, roused us in
   our sleep, the ballot-box opening grinned
and grinned again, gone we'd have been
                      could
   we have run . . . It wasn't we were stuck,
     stood frozen, transfixed, Paralytic Dream #12 . . .
It was waking known otherwise put running
   out of reach, nonsonance's waterless waves held
   us up, more than we could sense but
                       sensed

  even so, nonsonance's
 gaptooth
slur

   •

   Day late so all the old attunements gave
way, late but soon come even so . . . A
   political trek we'd have said it was
albeit politics kept us at bay,   nothing
                      wasn't
   politics we'd say. Wanting our want to
be called otherwise, kept at bay though
   we were, day late but all the old stories
                    echoed
yet again, old but even so soon come . . . A
   mystic march they'd have said it was,
   acknowledging politics kept us at
bay,   everything was mystical
they'd say. Wanting our want to be
               so
   named, kept at bay as we were,
              what
   the matter was wasn't a question, no
                ques-
  tion what
 it was

———————————

Nub no longer stood but lay and we
lay with it, earth-sway cradling our
   backs. What the matter was rocked
us, a way we had with dirt, awaiting
                              what
      already might have been there . . . Dust . . .
   Abducted future . . . Dearth Lake's dry
      largesse . . . Dread Lakes' aliases, alibis,
                                    Death
   Lake also there . . . Where we were rubbed
      earth in our faces, a feeling we had
         for debris. Nub, no longer standing,
      filled the air, an exact powder, fell
                              as
   we ran thru it, earth-sway swaddling
                                 our
   feet

Sound and Semblance

   —*"mu" twenty-sixth part*—

   A sand-anointed wind spoke of
survival, wood scratched raw,
   scoured bough. And of low sky
      poked at by branches,   blown
   rush,   thrown voice,   legbone
                           flute . . .
      Wind we all filled up with caught
      in the tree we lay underneath . . .
   Tree filled up with wind and more
                           wind,
      more than could be said of it said . . .
      So-called ascendancy of shadow,

branch, would-be roost, now not
   only a tree, more than a tree . . .

It was the bending of boughs we'd
  read about, Ibn 'Arabi's reft
ipseity, soon-come condolence,
                 thetic
  sough. We saved our breath, barely
                    moved,
   said nothing, soon-come suzerainty
volubly afoot,   braided what we'd
  read and what we heard and what
    stayed sayless,   giggly wind,
                wood,
  riffling wuh . . .   A Moroccan
   reed-flute's desert wheeze took
  our breath,   floor we felt we
   stood on, caustic earth we rode
across . . . It was Egypt or Tennessee
                we
  were in. No one, eyes exed out,
could say which. Fleet, millenarian
  we it now was whose arrival the wind
              an-
nounced

    •

  Night found us the far side of
Steal-Away Ridge, eyes crossed
  out, X's what were left, nameless
    what we saw we not-saw. We ducked
    and ran, rained on by tree-sap,
              dreaming,
chattered at by wind and leaf-stir,
   more than we'd have dreamt or
  thought. We lay on our backs looking
   up at the limbs of the tree we lay

underneath, leaves our pneumatic
                              book,
We lay on our backs' unceased reprise.

North of us was all an emolument,
   more than we'd have otherwise run.
   We worked at crevices, cracks,
      convinced we'd pry love loose,
                              wrote
      our names out seven times in dove's
                              blood,
      kings and queens, crowned ourselves
   in sound. Duke was there,   Pres, Lady,
      Count,   Pharoah came later. The
   Soon-Come Congress we'd heard so much
      about, soon come even sooner south . . .
                                        So
         there was a new mood suddenly, blue
                              but uptempo,
      parsed, bitten into,   all of us got our
   share . . . Pecks what had been kisses, beaks
      what once were lips, other than we
   were as we lay under tree limbs, red-beaked
                              birds
         known as muni what we were, heads crowned
                                        in
      sound only in
      sound

Dread Lakes Aperture

    —"mu" thirty-sixth part—

A wash of sentiment flooded frame,
ground, figure. The wall between
  "given" and "gone" grew thin, the
    dead surviving death in a swirl of
                          wind . . .
  "Children of the Night" was on
  the box. Wayne's nasal cry nudged
us on. We were them, their lapsed
    expectancy, gun barrel nuzzling
  the backs of our necks. "These
                children,"
we said with a sigh. Sat on grass
  eating something called poppin,
  sprung from an acoustic mirror,
suppositious canvas, prepossessing
  light . . . An elysian scene out of
                childhood
  almost, except the children sipped
beer, bourbon, wine. Spoke with
  mouths full, mouths wide open. We
saw poppin inside as they spoke . . .
                    Chuck
  E. Jesus they talked about going to.
  That or having gone, unclear which . . .
    Rude crew in whose childish guise
    our departed kin could again come
                  back,
these children were come-again elders,
  the elders were children again . . . These
children were drunk, dredged eldren, Drain
  Lake's namesake brew the beer they
  drank, drowned elegiac youth . . .

Light's bloom lay in disrepair, wounded,
lest it be called indulgent, earth prove
   overly lush. Sipped beer, bourbon,
                          wine,
  spoke with bubbles in their throats,
blew bubbles when they smoked
    instead of smoke. A meeting it
  seemed albeit angular, diffuse, a
                   rogue's
way with aspect, flecked. A synaesthetic
                       dance
  they could taste, called it poppin, hop
invading tooth, tongue, jaw . . . A great
   gift it seemed, bubbletalk ascending
    as it did even so. Brass rallied abject
reed . . . Dawn's colors came on without
                   warning,
  children of the night though they and we
were. Light's bloom was back or it was
   we were light-headed, lit heads loose
                 in a

   dream of
   light

———————————————

On a lit canvas what could've been
us, blown away. Was, andoumboulouous
  we, andoumboulouous they. Wasn't,
  andoumboulouous both . . . What to
   say: there was a was, there was a
                 wasn't.
  The vehicle we boarded held both, blew
up. What to say: there was an us, there
  was a them . . . The beginnings of
light, this was to say, abated, weakening
  glow begun to be said goodbye
              to,

flecked air fallen thru by motes . . .
Eye-squint, it went to say, went awry.
 "These children," we said, sucking our
      teeth. Newly come albeit chronic

                                    elders,
      reached out, drew back less than what
 was reached with, Nub it now was we

                                came
      to, tokens fell from the sky . . . Nub

                        was
      where we were, where we'd been,

                              where
      we'd be, chronic no
   less newly
 come

Suzanne Paola

Writing this statement has made me realize how little of a poetics I have, or how little anything I have resembles a poetics. I think my poetics, such as it is, is based on 1) laziness and 2) boredom. Once a poetry instructor I had told my class, "Keep revising. Once you get this poem written, the great thing is, you can write fifty more just like it." That struck me as poor advice, at least for a lazy person like me, since I would be writing redundant poems when I could be playing Legos with the kid or tending my undertended garden, and I would be bored to boot. To have the impetus to start a new book I need to feel there's something to do that differs from anything I've done before, and often that the present day has a light that needs to be let in. So *Lives of the Saints*, my most recent collection, is a political book because it was written at a very political time, and it would seem strange to turn away from days of petitions and protests to declare the world of poetry some kind of parallel universe, pure and disentangled.

When I was young, a high school dropout, I fell in love with both Wallace Stevens and Shakespeare. The Stevens came my way via a friend of a friend, and I read "Peter Quince at the Clavier" and "The Emperor of Ice Cream" over and over again. I had no idea what a clavier was, or what the poems "meant," or even why this was poetry, except that my body began to live through the poems—they set the rhythm for my thoughts and my pulse. I could recite those poems today, though I haven't read them in years. And the Shakespeare: I still hold my breath over the line in Macbeth saying, "The Queen, my lord, is dead." The entire play, the nihilism of the play, given to us in three brutal iambic feet. Without cause, without reason, without given names, there's life, there's death.

Tuscan Summer

Impossible to get used to it, this clarity.
Knowing the world, as God does, by its elements.
Light like a stiff lens, holding, delivering—
The small fury of a bird's flight, tattered fingers
balling and unballing into fists.
The stone, distant house, exhaling its dark breath into the pure—
How like drowning it is to love the world.
How close to danger, when the rocking
of what pulls us is endless, and salvation,
                        the little boat, squats
brooding in the green water, bow clasped,
                        light broken.

Calenture and Loom

> *Calenture: a tropical fever that caused sailors to mistake the sea for green fields, and jump into it.*
> *Loom: a phenomenon whereby solid objects appear to alter their shapes, occurring at sea.*

The sea at night looked simple from the shoreline.
Nothing we love is ever simple.

Therefore the songs we sang as we raised those sails
were songs of death and labor.

Therefore we hardened our hearts against the air.
And the sails luffed before swallowing the wind.

How can we ever forget such sweet oblivion?
Our lives on shore became just a few points of light

shining past the scarred persistence of the waves.
The dark winched in, star by star.

Phosphorescence beginning to stir in the ruffling water.
Motes of our childhood—do you remember—

Each row of houses an altar faltering before the moon.
Possibility bulked all around us in the singing air.

Crystal islands and ghost ships we could almost touch.
The slow, turning sparkle of the ferris wheel.

Our figures candled in the red glow of the starboard bulb.
Each slurred down to a form, a voice and pale light.

*

Now I wait alone for a hurricane to pass.
Inland, where things are always what they are

until we dream them away. Clouds hold the sky
behind the swollen knotting of their love.

Wind heaves and drags twigs and paper in its wake
as mountains toss and fall far distant.

But I can't stop looking
for the shapeshift seadark, the shivering wheel.

Those men who jumped to sea out of longing
for this hallucination, this earth—

Maybe it was fear of a water turned to dust,
held in the hushed breath of its own desire.

Maybe those sailors thrilled with joy to find,
instead of grass, the sea's all-forgiving flesh.

I remember it seeming wrong, somehow, to sit
in our wooden cup of air above its beauty—

How soft we could grow in that slow climate.
How low we would lie in those fields.

*

I imagine a world like this one, only deeper.
With the same occasional rages of the wind.

Spring sending its serpents' tongues along the branches.
A world that would be all light, or none.

We saw it, didn't we, brother, from the bow of our uncle's ship.
Laughed at the white bloom we cut from black water.

The rage that followed us into the cold morning.
Each day we rehearsed the lie called *family*

until we had it unflinching, and then it fell.
And what we thought protected us from the world

was the world, in all its clarity and edge.
Still, we relive those spilt evenings

when we gathered with our family at the edge of the bay.
And sailed, lashed together against the darkness.

The past is a spirit that never silences
until we bring it our souls, so we are born

and die there, where the white waits,
where we become what crashes endlessly into land.

The White

Snow drugs us to sleep
this evening. All one
suddenly, houses and lawns

one landscape.
The bare trees holding
a white, stunned fruit—
It feels like love.
Filling the gutters and the pipes,
blessing the cracked paint,
gilding the claws of the pecan trees.
Yesterday the old woman
at the subway lay as if waiting
for a lover,
curled up tenderly, hugging
her knees—
She smiled.
In her dreams,
each flake that touched her
was a grazing of lips.

I remember now how heroin
once made all of the faces kind.
Even the face of the black girl
giggling *She do stuff, don't she*
behind her hand at the 7-11.
At that moment she knew me
better than anyone, and I loved her
for that. And the small
coin of blood
in my palm from a dropped cigarette—
how it loved me, wanting
to stop bleeding.
The way the trees love us,
wanting to live again
under the snow, having already
seen the easier way, this whiteness.

Daphne

No end to the means of surrender.
        —Here the wind sweeping color into bent grass.
        —Here a god.

My footsteps sounding off the fullness of the earth and his
        parallel, echoing, echoing,
hurrying at mine, the way desire
hurries at its own image (must hurry)
as it escapes, as it always escapes.

Love would be the vanishing point
if we were able to contain the world . . .

If the honeysuckle could exist both as itself & its odor,
if the image didn't lie, so that even a god
can be fooled, I would kiss my damp spirit in your eyes . . .

Think of the moment
after seduction, the separation of bodies
into their spheres, each border
solidified by argument, the bed
a little world cut up by the gods
into domain & possession, into order.
The trivial *I,* the trivial *you.*

It seems my body is full of sex.
Bleeding & filling
& bleeding, like a tree tearing at its fruit.

—It's a lie I cannot be touched.

Each month, beautiful one,
I lose my heart.
From the surest exit, the darkest home.

Eros in Love

It wasn't hope or fear that drove her to see
But the long baths she took in his absence—
Steam rose like smoke from the paleness of the water.
She pictured her body burning; she couldn't help it.
The face she had never seen: would it know how to mourn her?
So she pushed him, sleep-sweet, into the light.

*

His were always apologies of a different order.
Always knowing what would happen, what did happen—
How she stood one morning under the flock
of gulls and the low clouds, each bird
absorbed in a few wingbeats into the white—
The tender image of death he shows the beloved.

*

She drew the curtains against the moon.
A greasy halo spread around the burning oil.
She imagined it rearing before her, all
the monstrosity of love, but there was nothing like that—
Just his goldfevered face, and the web of brilliance
holding them both in the godhead of its clarity.

Red Girl

A field. Huckleberry, vetch. The bees' thrum
a tongue of sound licking across it.
Each foxglove flower
choked with a small, trisected body
so the blossoms speak as insects.
A doe looks on. Amazed
at the voice her food has found, its tense, nonsensical
              insistence . . .

*

Under the pier, by glassy rocks, where the Puget Sound
licks its indecision—
arriving with a lunge, crawling out
& arriving—a gray seal
spins. Dead, intact, head caught
where the spume piles, so it's nodding
back & forth, saying *yes*, nodding, for as long as I can watch,
back & forth, *yes*. Exhausting
to see, this relentless agreement,
as if life is No, the capability of No.

*

And the Red Girl. Across
my street, all hesitant, afloat
in my field
of vision. Vivid
mote. Bright cell
in my study window. Cell with its mother's dress
pinned to its nine-year-old body.
An evening gown. Cut to fall
from the shoulders, so she pulls it
up-down, up-down, trying to fathom that. Her lips
smudged an arterial color, & the dress more alive
         even than that living red—

Flame scarf on her hair. Handbag. Evening shoes,
high-heeled sandals, in her arms.
She puts them on & stumbles for a while
as if someone has broken a small bone in each ankle.
Sits & holds
the rust-colored square of the bag
in front of her, a shield
for her lap, a dam there: says *No*
to you, silly seething world, & *No* to you, eye
in the window opposite, that watches me.

The Third Letter of St. Paul at the Playground

The deckle edge of sunset folds: a letter
sinks. You see that. Though nobody
writes to you & earth's just a hard ball
revolving. Everything
that is
is matter, even light:
or all matter's light (the wind
knocked out of it).

I look around.
I see packets of atomic
parts, each one
can go *boom boom* or assemble
into these sweet legs shimmying like geese gullets
over Barney sandals. Voices
from the swing caw Nah Nah Nah
Poopoo Head, or
peekaboo. A mother says *Destiny*
keep your socks on, so bored & chronic
her voice is like a vacuum sucking in.

She makes a tired wind with one hand.
& I can remember how hard it is
to wait like this, our microscopic parts
doing what they do, & we just umpires
in the game, not players really.
Do they put hard clots in the lung, does a burst
of atomic light knock us off the horse?
Stephen Hawking says space-time's curved
like the North Pole, a place where the child Destiny,
spinning to her bored mother, keeps lisping God lives.

Bin Ramke

A Poetics, of Sorts

Part of the fun of being alive is arranging and categorizing—a danger-
ous sort of fun, but it is part of being human. For instance, we think
of ourselves, we humans, as different from non-humans. Heidegger, in
Introduction to Metaphysics, says rocks are "worldless" (*weltlos*), the animal
is "poor in world, (*weltarm*)," and man is "worldforming" (*weltbildend*). I
have always liked this kind of quick system, but have always also consid-
ered such a system temporary, contingent—a poem. A poem is a system
for sorting: putting words and sounds and commas and semicolons and
whatever comes to hand into groups with connections.

"Sorting" is part of what we do with and to poems—establish genres. Or,
the poem can be a response to being out of sorts. The *OED* suggests that
"sort" as a verb implies a measure of randomness—it derives from a Latin
word meaning "to divide or obtain by lot." By chance. Poetry, to me, is
always and intimately connected with randomness, with unpredictability.
Poetry is what we have in lieu of explanation, and in place of consola-
tion.

Recently I used the word "shibboleth" in a poem—see somewhere in
Judges the story of that word's use to separate the outsiders from the in-
siders, and how its *meaning* ("ear of grain," or some say "stream") in the
denotative sense hardly matters. Mispronouncing the word meant death.
I often return (frequently against my will) to the Bible, when I look for

explanations of my own linguistic habits. Perhaps "accountings" rather than "explanations." And not only the Bible but the various rituals and readings of a religious childhood. Here is some of what such backward looking suggests: that early on I experienced language as "meaningful" but not as an information storage and delivery system; that words and sensory response could collude and form a new sort of meaning (cf. the taste of the wafer at mass, and the smell of incense, and the sound of the responses I was reciting by rote); that communities consist of isolated individuals who might speak the same words but had rarely the same feelings and thoughts, but speaking the same words gave them . . . consolation. Except I was not consoled.

The poem is always what happens when we think something else is happening—the poem exists always "in spite of," rarely because of . . . . Or at least this is true for me, and it is true for me both as reader and as writer. Language, and all the sounds we make whether language or not, suggests the shape of the inside of the skull. The mind. The brain's volutions and convolutions. The closest we can get to our own thinking is to attend to the words, the shapes our thoughts make as they escape. (I could, however, make a similar sort of case for any art, any application of individual notions of order to the received world—and I can make the case for mathematics, too—the shape thinking takes when it escapes the internal boundaries.)

The connection of writing to drawing, for instance, is significant and ancient. Poetry for me is not primarily about sound—at best, sound shares equal authority with the very look of words and lines and letters inked on paper (or shadowed on screens). The poem as physical thing, as extension into space, like the book as physical object, is beautiful in its efficiency and its ancient and its contemporary elegance. Poetry is an attempt to be aware of language as physical entity, and to make out of that awareness both elegance and intensity. Poetry is about what all physical things—including human beings—are about: the refusal to be something else; it is about the dignity of being.

As a maker of this stuff I have a suspicion that the making of poems gives greater pleasure than does the reading or hearing of them. Hence the ratio of manuscripts submitted for publication versus the number of printed books sold, for instance. But that is a story which takes us into the realm of poetry and economics, the poem as gift versus the poem as commodity. The concept of the Gift (see Marcel Maus via Lewis Hyde, Derrida, et al.) helps to account for much of the awkwardness in this particular historical moment of art in general and poetry in particular. We live in an era suspicious of gifts, an era which understands only reciprocal relations, which wants to have an accounting, a bottom line to everything, and it is a time which wants an end point to relationships. It wants the clarity that comes with language establishing limited meanings, with people knowing what they want, with sexes being well-sorted and stable, with national boundaries being clear and unvarying. The world has never been that way even when it is peopled by those who want it be so, and that is part of the delight of the world's gift of itself to us, *as* us. Poetry is a reminder of what "possibility" means. Poetry re-minds us, gives us again our minds.

No Thing

> *A word that is almost deprived of meaning is noisy. Meaning is limited silence.*
> —Maurice Blanchot

Sound as corruption is a further fall, a grace
like wind's incessant pounding, a music as anger—
air belligerent *versus* a single tree in a field
which is elegance as horizon as curtain drawn
against (any tree in singularity) light and light
whose nobility of patience penetrates the weather:
and from the air, from the airplane I saw
I saw beneath me during that time (I think it was time)
of year I saw the fall of leaves around each tree separate
a powdering of color pastel chalked circle a disk of leaves
and then red and bronze dots and then (we climbed)
the distant earth and then cloud and glitter
as soft in the distance like clouds among
cloud the tree speaking not to me only to itself like God.
Not silent. Nothing is. No thing like it except
surrounds itself with vibrating molecules
known as noise unless it is the susurrant leafage defiant
calling attention, calling. You recall, "Nothing
will come of nothing," said Lear to Cordelia.

The Gods That Sleep in Museums

Jorie Graham

It is cool and guarded. Godly.
The children are killing each other elsewhere
not here not among the marble busts and cenotaphs.

Under cover of daylight the dawn cowers—it is
only light innocent as anything a veil of seeing against
the glare of godliness the good like anger and
there *is* the integrity of shadow to annoy—there is
nothing for it in time this time of day—the dare.

A small mass of children seethes down
the street downhill hissing and spitting its way
past the louvered windows and shuttered
the small mass like cancer grows—No it is
only children otherwise called not history but

I have met a new and beautiful woman and
therefore the world makes a different sense
this morning she wears pearls a stringed instrument an
assortment of small smooth stones—she could
throw them the string could break the small
organically induced calcium deposits could
clatter like laughter onto the marble floor
small arcs degrading over time (bounce).

Eggs eyes riverstones rough roundness
of boulder gems cut and uncut

In a new calculation of risk we must
cast what small stones lie at hand
lying being the better part of valor
and fear being worse than fidelity bad as
bones—wings are another option cool and moist
unfolding gluey from the furred backs of moths
emerging into dark from the light of their soft eggs.

Somewhere in Gaza a boy opens both eyes
to the coming of the Prophet and grasps
a smallish stone igneous formed in
volcanic exuberance—to be the first the boy
to cast carefully this his small vote
against the national interest—his god
a small gnawing a dark egg of danger
which boys love boys live for like anything they do.

So here's the first lesson of history: hide.

The arc of each thrown stone confers
inevitability the tiny dance of fate the look
of numerical necromancy—once the stone leaves
the hand of the boy thrown in high spirit
a high arc a heraldry of itself

the stone is only acted upon is an agent of other
but might as well be its own universe it
falls fatal and full of significance

no god could be better served they clatter
small stones in the street the museum is shuttered

we are so lucky there is nothing called the past
we are so lucky we are a stone god is
another word for luck—for stone—for fear
the museum is the last refuge of refuge
it loves the little light the peace
the movement of stone upon stone
is a kind of burning.

Virtual Sculpture

There is no excuse for sadness consider
the starving the lilies the children of the field
who toil not neither are they happy.

She is one who brings the weight
of industrial ingenuity to bear on a small
object of art.

She is open to the world's suggestion
she will declare it when she sees it she selects
metal objects to subvert General Motors
into art foundering she places the cast off part
on a stone itself ecstatically chosen she
declares all is art in her small yard and I admire
the lines of silhouette, the delicate rust, the lingering there.

If she is also pregnant then she is two
and haunted by the opposite of ghost, the too
too solid and consider the tiny ocean there
the calm water less ocean than pool in which
the reflections of her face and flesh grow daily
Narcissus as mom, is, it is called expecting.

Is the future written in that pool which has
no surface a hand writing her hand or its it's
a found art a foundling castaway soon from its private
ocean, cast eros sore loser out.

Walking aimless I watched the children concern
themselves with history and the importuning of nations
no the casual arrogance of the world I noticed
the sunlight slanted against the bark of trees
the texture complex and the implications astounding
the boiling of biology along each limb a sculptural
announcing of itself the flesh the form the shape
casting the world and breaking the mold.

The Tender Grasses of the Field

When I was a saint I did not have visions but I could see and did note the
color of the world—mainly gray, variations on dirt. It's ok, you can live

here. The clean sky to attend the child whose hand is empty and mind is muddled.

Consider that earth is made of earth, a mineral and organic amalgam—beyond a tiny range, color is rare. Oh, they will tell you a particular plant, for instance, is red, that certain stars are red, but look for yourself. The color of fox, the color beneath the skin as platelets race, whirling alone in danger, for home.

What won't we do for the sake of the nerves, white threads of agony under the skin, on it, of it . . . in the wake of remorse we need to pronounce bigger than names. Maybe a verb. Every saint knew how to keep custody of the lips.

The view is lovely, nice sun going, a mountain it goes behind, the mountain made of rock and all. Et in Arcadia Ego, you know. A sheep here or there. A cow. Water. The sound of water if not water. The sound of sheep if not the smell. You call it home.

Where the Famous Wish They Had Lived

PARMENIDES OF ELEA

Where his influence could accumulate, where the horizon might retreat, where the basilisk smiles and the necessary arrogance of desire lingers into evening while yet hiding among the hieroglyphs. But I like it this way, he said to himself. Here shall I close my trustworthy speech and thought about the truth. Henceforward learn the beliefs of mortals, giving ear to the deceptive ordering of my words, he said. He watched stars move a certain way, the small sprinkling of the past he walked beneath when he was out late and lingering.

In a land of ha-has and paths of desire. Where Nothing hovers invitingly above the closest horizon. Between the angles of incidence and of reflection. Among the agonies in the garden. Elsewhere.

SIGMUND FREUD

"If his lips are silent, he chatters at his fingertips; betrayal oozes out of him at every pore." And yet looking into the mirror otherwise known as morning otherwise known as night was not a revelation to him. He had a path, strewn with candy wrappers, or flowers, and lined with stones, which was a comfort to him when his throat ached and his head betrayed him. Still wouldn't it have been good to stop in at some familiar coffee shop, to order in a childhood language a childhood treat, something with chocolate and a little something to soothe the guilt which follows from having hoped too fervently and made all those promises. A place where the libraries do not contain your own books and the children are not afraid. Memory, remember, is a dynamic process like the eloquence of birds and the kinds of cancer which affect the jaw. The cave of the mouth from which words emanate, and breath. "I am still out of work and cannot swallow," he wrote after the first of his thirty-three surgeries.

EMIL KRAEPELIN

"In dream I was a child—*childhood* is our myth of psychiatry, but children continue to live in dream—being chased across a landscape. I was not afraid—there is no fear in such landscape—but I did hurry. I would live there where there are no shadowy mountains, where rivers are slender gleams and cold, where the grasses vastly sound through the evening, sounding of air known as wind, felt—but there was a barrier, a glass wall under which a child's body might fit, but not his head. There is no child in this world but in the world of dream I want to live there, there on the other side. I want to live in someone else's dream, any healthy child's. I will live in any body."

Narcissus Old, Anyone Young

We were subtle dancers, this world and I,
when we were in love forever, ever
moving across the surface of
the other's eyes
                              resist this mirror's
glitter which keeps us intricate
and a little cruel but ready to gather
into arms an infinite remorse,

a sad seduction reduced into one last
smile a life spent waiting. With the slender tip
of her tongue in your ear, how can you listen?
  . . . and though beguiled be not betrayed   Lucretius

           There was a time we listened
like Echo, tried to be each the other,
learned to build cities and cemeteries, architecture
and architects, tried for order; in our intrigue never
guessed we could ever be other than lovers.

If only I could speak, what words I would say!
The surface of the pool wavers in wind, weaves
confluence into vision, into such humor
as the face which must be seen—
beguiling shiny hooks the fish seek out
hidden in shoals of littler fish hiding.

Pain is the History of Consciousness

We are at war we are told. There is a god of it.
Is there a god of pain? We are in pain. You are
welcome to your own. You may
protest. A small bird—passer—

passes my window and its shadow
across the drawn shade is like a drawing
I once in better times displayed.

The light is a kind of passing like pain.
At war, and in light, and the bird flies
specter-like past my window which is luxurious
and full of future. Like an omen
a body is a poor excuse. Impoverished.

You know, pain. A war
rewards all small affairs. Air
and apples abound in this district,

166 · *Bin Ramke*

happily for our comfort. We miss most
the small warmth of afternoons.
Recall a tidy elegance, specter of
when one was happier reading hints of what
to expect when the body bent unwilling—bends
unwilling to its task. Pain is
arrogant, dismissive, debonair.

After Virgil

All through the precise butchery lungs
retained much of the last breath of the bull
like light waiting in candle wax—even when
tossed onto the altar there was the chance
to return to sound, song, lament,
a bellow of desire a residue of despair.

Chemical Virtue

Swiss violet, Methylene blue—names limit the languor of this world,
its agony called appetite. You eat it, it changes color. You breathe it, it
warms, returns to its turbulence more human, more anxious to please.
Or so we, heroic and altering, wish. I like knowing something, but much
is too much. When I learned that the shape of a protein was how other
proteins knew to attach, I recognized the romance. She, walking toward
me accidental on the sidewalk, has a shape. *Pluck from the memory a
rooted sorrow* the man said—it was a question, can't you, or why can't
you. . . . Erasure is the great desire, chemical and candid. Take and eat,
this is my body. I noticed how neatly the clouds fit into those holes in the
air, then I thought how the air is part of the cloud so there is no hole, just
more of the same. And the sun breaks itself into little pieces which hurtle
my way, enter my face through the lens, a little piece of me like water. It
all becomes the Egyptian art decreed evil by Diocletian, chemistry, the
old writings treating of silver, gold, and transformation; the darkness of
the earth which is fruitful, even to excess, contrasts with the light color
of desert sand, barren and beautiful. The name of a thing is the history

of the thing—or the name and the history is the thing. Or, what does a
boy want with history, such a toy, a chemistry set in his basement, a little
Bunsen burner of his own alight, flickering, a golden hue against the wall,
holy the vision.

Been There Done That (Desert Warfare)

Pluck from the memory a
rooted sorrow the man said—it was
a question, can't you, or why
can't you . . . . Erasure is the great
desire, chemical and candid.
Take and eat, this is my body.

I noticed how neatly the clouds fit
into those holes in the air, then I thought
how the air is part of the cloud, too,
so there is no hole, just more of the same.
And the sun breaks itself into little pieces
which hurtle my way, enter my face
through the lens, a little piece of me
that is like water. If in a desert an airplane
were to descend from clouds—not this cloud,
but like this, this shape, this chemistry—
it could be like a memory, fitted
into a whole a hole in the brain
the cloud-shaped brain. A world fits there,
a small, damaged world.

For the Relations of Words Are in Pairs First

> For the relations of words are sometimes in oppositions.
> For the relations of words are according to their distances from the pair.
> —Christopher Smart, fragment B, 4

Hear, and here is where it is spoken; some say
and sum up a kind of catalogue of self, a self
is a catalogue of lacks, some say as a catalogue of likes,

of nostalgias—
what was once and will not be won again
over the usual couplings in the night
against the light continue even this
                              this night, tonight
these words are written; the rain
a spilling of kindness, a kind spell.
                              Tantrum?

Donald Revell

Dear Friend,

I must start by telling you I can never think of Poetry as anything but a loving power, a god who sometimes visits me and visits you along its bright unfolding way. It seems quite fine to me that Jack Spicer called these visits "dictations," and equally fine that William Blake should choose words like "Everlasting Gospel." A poem is the efflorescence of a power, evidence of something whose purpose is, I truly believe, our happiness and even our delight.

And so invited to offer advice to poets younger than myself, I choose a text whose pretext is just such a happiness: powerful, sudden, and shared. I'm saying I carry a poem in my pocket. It's not a mantra or a model. It's good news and evidence. These days, it's a later poem of William Carlos Williams's—"Iris":

a burst of iris so that
come down for
breakfast

we searched through the
rooms for
that

sweetest odor and at
first could not
find its

source then a blue as
of the sea
struck

startling us from among
those trumpeting
petals

All the reminders and advice I could hope to share are here. (And, of course, elsewhere—always a good idea to change the poem in your pocket to remember poetry never changes.) And so, again, to begin:

A poet, whatever else he or she may be, is not a creative writer. As Emily Dickinson opined, "Unto the Whole—how add?" The world creates itself, and poetry is pleased to show its new creation to our words. Williams's "burst of iris" is the author of the poem. What Williams writes is the record of its authority and of his coming to his senses, all of which lead to an iris.

And so, clearly, there's no need for imagination. It would be a downright hindrance. The poem is entirely of its real place and moment. Nothing is missing which imagination might supply. Write where you are. Our art is simply one form of attention, a going out to meet the world that comes so freely, so effortlessly to us and to our senses. It would be an effort not to smell the "sweetest odor," an effort not to seek its "startling" source. Imagination is just such an effort, and who needs it as long as there are flowers?

Always welcome distraction. Remember Baucis and Philemon. They were eternally rewarded. Williams's poem is one delighted upshot of distraction, something much better than the breakfast for which he'd come downstairs. You cannot come to your senses by closing your ears and eyes. Poets don't need retreats; they advance. Poetry is a wild god, and our piety consists of an always grateful bewilderment. (I love the 17th-century form of bewildered, i.e., bewildernessed!) To be amazed, one must enter, willingly if unintentionally, a maze. Think of the first line of John Ashbery's "Some Trees": "These are amazing." And God knows what prolixities "Kubla Khan" might have sunk beneath without the blessed haphazard of a person from Porlock. After all, it was the same Coleridge who found himself redeemed by distraction in his great "Dejection: An Ode." A raving wind blew him out of his mind and into the next valley, where he was loved. Leave the window open. Answer the door. Catching the fragrance of a flower, go and find it.

I come to a plain distinction, and there, I find, is everything I know about being a poet. There is mind, and there is mindfulness. Throw away your mind; it is a ragbag of wishes and words. Mind can only recognize the wearing and worn-out measures of itself. If you find yourself in a cave, you needn't unpuzzle the shadows on the wall. Turn yourself round and walk into the sunshine making them. I forget what wonderful American preacher it was who once said "If you find you're rubbing the cat the wrong way, turn the cat around." Whoever he was, he knew a very great deal about Poetry. He was mindful. Mindfulness has eyes and can be surprised by joy. It can find an iris.

Motel View

It is conceivable in fact that waves
and luster work in such a way, in such
a mannered disproportion, that the sea
becomes an architectural conceit
with which to play upon the measure of
a liquid give and take, a weathering. Wave
and the measurement of it can therefore do
but little to intensify the spume
of water in the sun. Cape Ann today
is seascape, rock, and a freezing wind. The moon
is nearly full, but risen far too soon
to have its proper place in the postcard, sun-
light being quite the thing for photographs,
the elderly, and a decent view of the gulls.
(When thinking back, it is the elderly
that one remembers most, enclosed by gulls
and glaring eastward like the benches.) Wave
and luster mannered to a fault, the cold
vacationland in April, all combine

into a law of things, an intellect
of various disproportions, which, by day,
can sometimes contradict the weather, give
one's time a fiction, or, as water does,
an elemental dullness, an expanse.

Raft of the Medusa

Some things are even more important
and we point frantically in that direction
toward the vertical music of landfall.
Think of us, then, as the huge victims of shipwreck
revived in the tall studio of a painter
in north light. We are never bigger than that.
And we are overshadowed even then
by some things taller, far inland with our houses.

No sense putting the blame on Géricault.
A man's sheer size is no bigger than his death
no matter if he is painted as a giant
among other giants on a cannibal raft.
You need to look away from the north light.
You need to find drowned men small and living
inland in the shady use of affection
for things deathless for no reason.

That is where you find things more important
than shipwreck. Among the rafts of light novels.
In corners of windowseats that look down
onto the front walk between dark leaves
folded like messages. A long time
before anyone is shipwrecked, he has chosen
part of a novel or some green window
never to die, never to let him die.

He is eaten on the raft of the Medusa.
Or he drowns in aftertimes in a tilted bed

beneath the cannibal comforts of dry land.
The north light shows up nothing of this. The tall
studio of the painter is too busy
with corpses pointing frantically in one direction
towards a vertical music he does not paint—
a folded message deathless for no reason.

Survey

I am so lonely for the twentieth century,
for the deeply felt, obscene graffiti
of armed men and the beautiful bridges
that make them so small and carry them
into the hearts of cities written like words
across nothing, the dense void
history became in my beautiful century.
When a man talks reason, he postpones something.
He gets in the way of a machine that knows him
for the sad vengeance he is, somewhere close
to the bald name of his city. "New York"
means "strike back." "Attica" means "strike back"
and so does any place in the world
in the huge eyes and tender hands of my century.

I went to the capital. I had a banner
and there were thousands of people like me.
There was an airplane, and for a moment
heavy with laurel and sprays of peach blossom
something that had never happened before
stretched like a woman's shadow on a hedge
between the plane and the people who saw it flying.
It was the real name of the century.
It told everyone to strike back
until there was no reason in the world
except a machine stalled overhead
that knows everyone and is as delicate
as peach blossom. But the poor years come too late.

Apocrypha

I don't know why anyone writes history.
The vertical, thin-ankled civilizations
of morning, the evening continents
just now taking their soft hands away
from the bodies of men killed in rioting,
from the close, deluded eyes of one woman
whose angels knew none of Paradise,
whose physicians put her body in the ground—
what good are such things? Where are their teeth?
The heart bites down and scarcely knows itself

or the small, coral woman beside me
who would give her heart to the map on the wall
more easily than to gods in love with games.
The hillsides just beyond her window flower
in bright patches more generous than laughter.
The air is a clean residence and airplanes
buoyant overhead. A man in the next apartment
types out the name of a lost continent. He types
the names of its kings and the long rites by which
they became kings. He betrays each secret

in its turn, and broken characters
caper to the margins of his page, not suffering
because he has suffered enough for them all.
Gods begin with secrets, as do kings and history
and the mistake of pain. When I am with you
the temples draw into themselves like evening
beneath bright patches of the mock orange.
Or they do not, and I am in the teeth
of the faithful on the temple stairs, thrust
into the ground with bad angels and bad physicians.

Their gods were too much in love with games.
It was too much like suffering, spilling
out of temples, multiplying
into the less admirable bodies of laughter,

little flowers the size of your thumbnail
dividing hillsides and the air into so many
loving fragments that the temples died
of increase. I knew a man who died in the rioting.
I know a woman who mistook those flowers
for the ascent of angels and pure physicians.

Wartime

All the more beautiful in the concert hall
with people in their fine clothes and yourself
in the same place as the original music.
The rest, I imagine, must be like the sound
of a radio orchestra in the nineteen-forties,
Europe fiddling beneath the darkness,
and those abandoned in the capital cities
leaning into the sound as it becomes noise.

Our lives seldom advance. And the beautiful
is a principle either too large
or too small to contain so much loose
and indispensable striving.
That is why I think of music, why I love
even the idea of an orchestra
in the open spaces of the outdoors
and worried corners of room during the blitz, my love's last hours.

They do not move much, but they are real.
They live in the anticipation
and in the backwards aftermath. They feel
light canceling the illumination
of the previous moment when I told you
Europe was dead. Mahler already knew.
That is why I said that being inside of you
is the harsh Symphony and withdrawing from you

a song at the end, something of the earth
too large for desire, too small to survive.

And these analogies are still nowhere
close to you, close to me, who are trying
so hard to believe that things
are not the hallucinations of bad history
or of autumn settling into its long self-pity
of mists and overripeness apt not to change.

In early November, the city parks hum
beneath the thinnest frost. The couples
and solitaries have got it wrong at the
lake's edge, feeding the birds, saying
nothing to themselves or to each other
about the coming holidays, the anticipation
buried close by, in the wrong place perhaps,
but someplace. It fills the earth like music.

The Massacre of the Innocents

The law moves quickly in the rain
and chokes the world with memorials.
The courts accept the lowest superstition
into evidence. And we embrace quickly in the rain,
conceiving a hale infant with hands to wrinkle
the bedsheets toward it, wave by trough by wave.

We had the autumn. We had an hour
of massacre and then the wintertime.
I am beginning to believe in Fate,
in the circulation of ash inside
the bone, clattering along the pavements
like yellow shrapnel. It needs no purpose.
It needs only an engine and a name.
When you open a child, there is nothing
but a cramp of terror and a wrinkling hand.
In the unannealment of autumn, autumn shatters.
In a crow's mouth, love is a crow's mouth,
and the white percussion of faith is all the sound.
I heard it—white percussion like pianos

striking pianos, and no outrage, no transport.
Murder wrinkled its hand inside my house
that is my house no longer.

Man is weakest.
Faith chokes the world with his memorials.
Unbelief chokes the world with his nakedness.
There is no future if the past is helpless.
Let it find engines equal to these bones.

Anniversary of Many Cities

Darkness undrew the air where it was naked,
poppy and dramaturge, flower and firebomb.
Too much innocence survived.
Something remnant, twilight without end
on the receding cockpits, tainted
the alcohol of orphancy. Every wall
was a shafthouse, every plume of smoke a woman
lewdly photographed by her kinsmen.

I live on credit.
I love a man, and he is meat.
I love a woman, and she is red hair,
a plume of smoke who loves me longer.
All over Europe, restorations proceed
and make a sound exactly nothing, a tone
between a whine and a detonation.

Whoever minted the coin of total war
made everything else worthless, counterfeit.
Take it to the madhouse or take it to bed,
it is still war. Getting and spending
are war. Because there is no such thing
as immortality, sufficient unto the day
are its casualties.
What does not die deserves to live.

Inquire

The god is how many
bridges and automobiles
cut off mid-sentence
in the effect of style?

Week and eerie with
distance like all
magic, scattered,
commingled and gone,

the god persists in
the singing before
the syringes of waking.
He is the pause endlessly.

He breaks the tree,
and it waits to fall.

Once Divided

In prayer, the open hand
collapses. The surface
of the lake is nearly
ice, and even without
it the wind destroys
silence in the only tree.

In my open hand, winter
eludes the exact center.
On shore, the heron is ice.
In flight, the heron is
a cloud between the lake
and a crescent moon.

The water does not freeze.
The moon withdraws into

the frozen air. Something
exactly mine arises
in like efforts and lake-
effects and dies there.

Mechanics

What neighborhood? Only death and trees, or one
Tree. Someone explained to me the difference
East from West is the imagination
Of a single tree as against a forest.
Was he smiling? The Californians settle
Like a gold ash upon their pine woods.
A stone's throw west of Melville's tomb, my father's
Headstone tilts under one spruce kept alive
By sprinklerheads and a Puerto Rican gardener.
The gardener sings in the accent of his ocean.
At Big Sur, there are too many sounds to count one.
The forest is endless. A tree is almost none.
This is the house that Jack built East to West.
He was smiling, and his teeth were planted in rows.

Martha Ronk

Poetics of Failure

In his book *In Quest of the Ordinary,* Stanley Cavell states, "The everyday is what we cannot but aspire to, since it appears to us as lost to us." I have tried to create poems that read in a seemingly temperate and straight-forward manner, but that unsettle the reader by intense, shifting, or confused focus, by a swerve toward the unexpected even if highly recognizable. The "quotidian" seems somehow a possible counter to skepticism, a check on self-involvement and a refusal to admit that there is anything other to confront than oneself. Such poetry has the potential to map and blur the ground between self and world, past and present, local and abstract. It can reach for the uncanny, can approximate something both ordinary and utterly odd, in an alternation and oscillation that maintains both. This liminal space may appear, for example, in the arena between two images such that the eye/mind moving from one distinct image to another finds itself in a transitional space that undoes, unhinges, opens, slips. I am per-force drawn to the visual. In Lee Friedlander's book, *Black/White/Objects,* there are two juxtaposed photographs, one of a man of wood (a crucifix) and one of a man of air (a balloon manikin in a Macy's parade). As one's eyes cross back and forth from the image on the left to the image on the right, one's mind flutters, not only seeing the two as one, not only over-lapping them, but also not being able to do this. The operation fails and in this splendid moment of failure, tied by slender thread to success and the released spark of juxtaposition, I would hope to locate my work.

One can also think to create this space by using, as I have been lately, the words of someone else, as if there were at least two lines of language, spooling simultaneously, affecting one another and creating new meaning in ways not entirely spelled out or articulated. The words of many poets serve as models for me, but lately, the author who has had most influence is W.G. Sebald. Part of the reason is that his emphasis on the failure of eyesight and memory overlaps my own. My recent work, *Vertigo*, takes its title from one of his novels and tries to capture what it means to be shattered out of the normative. Another alignment between his novels and my poetry is that his work often includes references to (or actual, if out-if-focus) photographs as proofs and as failed proofs of what was there. Photographs often gather up a framed prolific world that seems both artificial and given (think of the jumble of stuffed dolls, manikins, corsets, posters in storefront photographs by Walker Evans or Eugene Atget). From Sebald's *Austerlitz*: *Even when I glanced up from the page open in front of me and turned my gaze on the framed photographs on the wall, all my right eye could see was a row of dark shapes curiously distorted above and below-the fixtures and landscapes familiar to me in every detail having resolved indiscriminately into a black and menacing cross-hatching. At the same time I kept feeling as if I could see as clearly as ever on the edge of my field of vision, and had only to look sideways to rid myself of what I took at first for a merely hysterical weakness in my eyesight. Although I tried several times, I did not succeed.*

The restless question, "why," stands for me at the center of poetics: questioning why things are as they are, why standardized versions dominate: insisting, suspending, moving into fluidity and failure. My book, *Why/Why Not*, focuses on a series of Hamlet-like questions-since his "to be or not to be" stands at the center of the book-and then on a series of flippant responses of someone like Ophelia, irreverent, crazed. As the play moves to its conclusion, Hamlet also uses and accepts failure; his statement before the final death scene is analogous for me to a version of negative capability: "There is special providence in the fall of a sparrow. If it be now, 'tis not to come; if it be not to come, it will be now. The readiness is all. Since no man, of aught he leaves, knows aught, what is't to leave betimes? Let be." My work exists in the interrogative mood, whether or not a question mark appears at the end of a line.

I try for language that is familiar and yet in which words are juxtaposed in unusual ways, for sentences that seem quite ordinary, but veer off in new directions, take up unexpected threads, omit transitions. I jam two sentences together so that certain words fall out, leaving a trace despite their absence, operating even as memory operates, catching hold and failing. It is complex syntax that must do most of the work, the articulation between one sentence and another; I am not interested in single words set in white space, but in joinery. Like others, I am wary of narration, but am also interested in the complex integuments of a line, and in music as part of that complexity. I want to catch the threads of transitory things, to acknowledge the dislocation we all suffer and count on. Or perhaps I'd be more honest to say I can't help it. I have tried to write about an exuberance I admire, but find myself constantly drawn to the fragility of all things in the face of time, to the transitory, to what the Japanese call *aware*. I don't think of this melancholy, however, as anything I would prefer to do without.

In much of my work I have focused on place, not only daily and private places, but also the larger place of the city I live in, Los Angeles. Place is often a site both of memory and of history, and place has been used historically to produce images, language, sequences, memory itself. LA, for example, is a place in which coming undone is vivid (the desert is about to take over, dust descending on a fragile if hyperbolic civilization); buildings are often make-shift and decaying before being finished (as in the photos of Lewis Baltz); languages are multiple and mixed; the unsettled pervades subject matter. One proposition I would put forward is that the west often seems to cross boundaries and to foster work that breaks, disrupts, alters genre, shifts from poetry to prose or prose to poetry, from narrative to the journalistic, from music to obvious "noise," from the textual to a representation of orality (the spoken).

Failure—or, to use a specific rhetorical term, apophasis—is fruitful one might say. It is fruitful for me because it allows an assertion or emphasis by pointedly passing over, ignoring, or sliding by it. Instead of writing by means of analogy or even juxtaposition, one can write by means of a segue that allows items to glance by one another, to relate by tangential or even detached images. Often for me this "failure" occurs in the tension between the visual and the verbal, an interest that comes perhaps from my studying that very tension in Shakespeare's work. As they belie one another, shatter one another, they also, potentially, suggest and enhance. The whole seems to teeter and to fail, certainly to defy logic, but in the most satisfying moments, in the failure of absolute congruity, to create new constructs.

Reading Sappho

Of course her thighs, of course the way she gasps
when some Spartan strolls languidly by. Of course
she can't get enough of skin. Days later you delay

telling me how beautiful the words are, how sweaty
they make your palms. You remind me how you
respond after the fact. Watching your thin beauty

I recall Sappho's full lips, the plenitude
of her smile. She imagines women with multiple legs
jumping into the cosmic sea. Water fills up with them.

We walk a tightrope. If the time is right
we wonder whether we should say what's on our minds.
Your hair is fine-lined, my fingers knotty bone.

The flesh of Greek women fills the room. We leave
thin wrists behind, cross out whatever is written
about us. A fat woman stoops to fasten a strap.

Elgin Marbles

Their shoulders lie back in their sockets, they
insist on warmth, throw off drapery; their skin
looks hot. Innocent, uncouth,
they ask all of us to come touch them,
pull off their marble clothes.

Once

I saw a shoulder like that on a girl

larger than her age who knew how to come on,
disdained anyone who'd lay a hand on her.

Blouses the color of naked skin, she cut
her hair completely off and sat
absolutely still: no one could touch her.

                   This time
in the vast hallway when the guard's back
was turned, I put my hand on the shoulder
of someone whose name is not known for sure.

Still life: to name, to want

They thought to name themselves: basket of,
fruit and, the pipe, the peach, the pane.
Someone is looking out of, her bouquet fails.
One looks like a cupboard, open, dangling
its keys; inside there is music written out
on paper, two books, what looks to be jam.
The lid shuts forever. No one will get in
but the invitation will suggest itself,
insinuate, obsess, and our longing will grow
over time for wanting to get in, get in,
not the cupboard, not even the frame.
No one even reaches the room the painting
is hanging in, the hallway, the door, the room.

[If I say I don't believe you is this impatience]

If I say I don't believe you is this impatience
without waiting for an answer which might take days or years.
Hard to sit still to hear what in the interstices might sing.
Again that liquid bird repeating the same story
over and over in the car as you list the placements
of adjectives and verbs out of which arises what seems

to be music in the malleable and soft folding of silver
inside an afternoon parenthesis of what was it again?

[The paragraph she gives me to live in is I don't know how]

The paragraph she gives me to live in is I don't know how.
Description is a phenomenon of walks as obvious as rain.
All the outcroppings in a brownish moss I can't get over
the undulations of columns through which the distance
is an extension of how we think someone walks.
She says you are where you should have begun.
She offers copses and seclusion,
bitterns crying in the lintels.

Ophelia over the pond

Considering everything the deliberation is queasy
and the dizziness abruptly coming
and the peculiarity is foursquare upon us
and the vacancy of the vast afternoon.
It is very true what they say about the difference
between an hysteric and a saint.
It is all very well and good what they say is coming.
What is required by the very nature of the characters involved
and the tone of the situation which makes it tentative
and right then and there in a misapprehension
or the acrid smell of her wet hair.

Why knowing is
(& Matisse's Woman with a Hat*)*

Why knowing is a quality out of fashion and no one can decide to
but slips into it or ends up with a painting one has never
seen that quality of light before even before having seen it

in between pages of another book and not remembering who knows
or recognizing the questionable quality of light on her face
as she sits for a portrait and isn't allowed to move an inch
you recognize the red silk flower on her hat
and can almost place where you have seen that gray descending
through the light reversing foreground and background
as the directions escape one as the way you have to
live with anyone as she gets up finally from her chair
having written the whole of it in her head as the question
ignored for the hundredth time as a quality of knowing is
oddly resuscitated from a decade prior to this.

ARROYO SECO

The gap in logic cuts a dry riverbed across the land
unerring in inference and what follows from what isn't there
eroded about the edges of metaphor
where redwood and imported palm catch a glimpse
of the new world. So much remains unseen
despite the broad view or the absence of foliage
rolling down to the arroyo which from a certain vantage
appears swallowed up by point of view.
Drawn to it as drawn to the pointlesness of it all
after a while I couldn't tell if nostalgia was
for a place or a time or before learning to think.

NOT KNOWING THE LANGUAGE

A tendency towards mannerism and widening the streets
into vacant lots dotted with waxed paper.
Not knowing the language mixes them up.
Her wasn't in it, her pulse said no.
Too easy to erase what from the perspective of the bird
might be *mala suerte* or flying on the left hand
before the entrails were opened in the sun.
Reading the fortunes of those caught in forces
beyond the control of waiters studying to be polite
or policing the small turns of phrase
might get them to forget what the future holds.

NEUTRA'S WINDOW

Behind the glass barrier by moving her lips
a woman forms exhortations. Her mind is made up.
What shadows of silence under eucalyptus
where the absence of mirrors protects children
and breaks relentless cycles of words.
Fingers over lips in early portraits marks the mastery
of silent reading, a conclusion of mouth begun by all
who suck out conclusion from the ragged spill
of palm and encumbent dust. The child reads her mind.
Silently and with the stealth of figures pilfered from story
one escapes dominion.

THE MOON OVER LA

The moon moreover spills onto
the paving stone once under foot.
Plants it there one in front.
She is no more than any other except her shoulders forever.
Keep riding she says vacant as the face of.
Pull over and give us a kiss.
When it hangs over the interchange
she and she and she. A monument to going nowhere,
a piece of work unmade by man. O moon,
rise up and give us ourselves awash and weary—
we've seen it all and don't mind.

THEY SAY IT MIGHT RAIN

Commentary is underdone.
Birds make meaning all morning
dying by sound alone.
A red roof is tearing its throat
and each insect abuzz in the room
shrinking around each moment of skin
as the photograph brings them out all night long.
The yellow reaches all the way to the room
arrives by airmail or express.
She walks as upright as ordinary beauty

and indexes everything exactly the same.
They say it might rain.
You can't miss the sound of rusty machinery
even when I can't remember my voice.
Washing is one dish, one shirt,
something not metaphysical
and one chair to hang it on.

THE FOLDING SCREEN

Then the screen was folded up and taken to the top of a hill
where the egg marked with blood balanced on a nail.
All the guineas made feathers and made the folding up of wings
and the screen once behind glass in a far off museum
where fingers pointed to the bamboo and the peacock's tail
was folded and put away for a winter when the winds would blow
and every exposed wrist would freeze before you got back
and the trees would clatter in ice and the ground disappear
and remembering the silk would become as distant as eyes
clouded over it was then early summer and the rains came.

ARS POETICA

It's enough perhaps not to go anywhere.
The stream disappears into the upper regions of the scroll
or the credits come on at an angle more arresting
than the film as whole which is a dead-end bit about rain.
Moving through the countryside without a path
without lifting a finger or looking to the future
the monks are framed by a circle of cloud
the girl by a stray hair falling across her brow
wet from the downpour in which everyone is speaking French
in a mad dash for cover.
One of them gazes through centuries at a cloudburst.
The girl's gone to study revolution in Prague.
At another turn enlightenment comes of walking rough terrain
and the girl's in love again and speaking French.
The poet keeps reading from right to left.

A Photograph of a Plate Glass Window

We come to know ourselves through these photographs
as if they were memories yet to come.
An act of mortification looking at the boy in his arms
not the essay about the light off the plate glass (the bird flying into it)
not learning to keep quiet.
The face out there is the one I used to walk by the store
near where I lived. The items in the window, the curtains I'd forgotten.
The boy in his arms was a boy.
The way one no longer has anything to say looking at (the bird flying
     into it).
The wings expand, we say, the wings are expanded in a blue light.
He writes an essay about it and disappears into the future
of photography where the boy used to lie in his arms.

Some Birds

Life's approximate is how someone might have put it
and I think that's sort of true.
It's the monotone moved from one tree to another just a bit further
     down the road.
I sort of study birds he says, I too had a life in the years before
and then there were more years added and it just seemed to go on.
Migration takes some from the far north to the coast of Mexico before
     they begin again.
Their wings are narrower, their tails forked
but the note from the tree I've never heard it before.

After Watching Jules et Jim

The water keeps lifting over the watery weeds.
Without a thought in the world is what we say about the things of this
     world.
Meantime and meanwhile I can't help it.

What is it with these enigmatic smiles
and have you tried that on anyone else.
Also what works in one place doesn't necessarily work in another.
The water keeps lifting over the weeds as the weeks go by.
Now is it today and then it was the film we were watching in French
and her maddening but enigmatic smile.
We walk mindlessly through the weedy water
though the ending of the film was far more dramatic than that.

> *The line which ought to be a line between the sea and sky obscures*
>   *itself badly.*
> *It's a messy job but someone has to do it.*
> *If one wants things in place, a girl who's beautiful and good*
> *it's no good watching French films.*

A failing memory

She began to remember in random bits, the years having
gone by in a habit of desultory reading, books open 78, 79,
couldn't any longer call up the entire system once so clear
and wasn't it the method of the rescue but she found herself
trying to see as a bird from overhead to get the lay of the land
the way the maze had been laid out and planned
but then after the wings and beak,
the hanging feet and bits of broken shell
and after thinking through the float itself
from its edges into the slightly moister center, she lost it
and though she knew the labyrinth had been somehow significant
it seemed to fade before the corner of a page,
the quotation folded down on itself,
and then there was the envelope marked Montreal,
she thought she might have remembered Montreal
at this distance less so and instead the corner of a page
and the storefront in Albany, the skeleton of a leggy bird.

Aaron Shurin

Some Measure

Who I want to be or think I am in fancy; how the world should make justice shine; the revelatory power of what (I think) you ought to know: Oh I'm a foolish Puck, why trust me? My shenanigans equal my noble sentiments; emotion crowds my scrupulous invention. All I wanted to say—*all I thought to give you*—is contradictory, speculative, moment. Standing on this shifting ground (San Francisco fault lines) requires the precision of attention I'm calling today the complexities of measure.

Grandiloquence makes sense to me most times I look at the sky, so I'm not afraid of Romantic gestures. [At least I'll do things in writing I wouldn't *wear*, for example—and I probably wouldn't wear the sky—though I did just buy a midnight blue tunic with azure panels that I thought daringly acceptable but my boyfriend kindly acknowledged with very faint praise.] I mean language leads me into places I'd otherwise fear to go. Yesterday a student listed for me all the things he hated to do in writing. That's his lesson for next week, of course. What revelation is he afraid of? Disjunction, interference, multifoliation, "swoony music": my senses proper.

If I knew myself too well I probably wouldn't write, but I'm a sleeper. I'm drawn to writing poetry to keep me awake. I'm not a model of action, I'm not of princely behavior, but I know what sweet song is, and I can rock you to sleep with it, I'm a sleeper. But the sweet song is also the morning lark's: wake up! Contradiction is the synchronic view of a dialectic.

I'm interested in the utilization of both poetic and narrative tensions: the flagrant surfaces of lyric, the sweet dream of storied events, the terror of ellipsis, the audacity of dislocation, the irreversible solidity of the past tense, the incarnate lure of pronouns, the refractability of pronouns, the simultaneity of times, the weights and balances of sentences. I'm interested in lyric's authenticity of demonstration and narrative's drama of integration; lyric, whose operation is display, and narrative, whose method is seduction. I describe a set of binary terms across which I see writing passing an exchange of values, and it becomes a multiple texture/text—writing in just those created tensions between surface vocalic tangibility and referential transparency; between theme and emptiness, measure and interruption, the eternal present and past of memory/future of dream: all present, all heightened, operational.

The shadow letters dance on a choral ground. Organization of sound in its textual skin is poetry's purest pleasure, measure's measure.

Subjectivity, oddly enough, proposes community, so I'm led by my nature and particular history to the imagination of "person" as the heart of the nexus. If the drama has a body I understand where I am better, and I carry in mine the idea that images are the poem's erogenous zones. But willfulness—we can call it intentionality—does not drive the car: by and large my subject is the vehicle to whom experience happens. Composition's a reflexive art: deliberate surrender. Form is a set of accidents whose tension resembles coherence.

What the poem permits me to make is the meaning I'm after. There's a precision of attention that clarifies relations, and when the phonemes slide I'm in heaven.

A's Dream

Here's where I came in, captive and their speeches. Anxious like any new moon, days away will be filled with dreams. From the main image its mood passing through its phases, a different mind immediately disrupted. Two will run between love and law. Her eyes must learn to see another's eyes. In the thrill of the wind shadows turn the pillars into trees. Flee the swirling house, free the following night. It rains on you, shaken to the horizon line.

*

Beams can mislead as well as lead, spell out transforming mind. Great poignance shed tears of their own audience. Some floral names seem as if they're part of another dimension. Sensing an opening the cattle are feeding off drowned roses; what kind of boy is a changeling? He uses personification just as people do. With X lurking in the unseen air how safe would you feel? Approaching voices are heard. He's interested in finding them, not in dealing with them.

*

The way things should be change places with sentimental remorse. Likes to sleep there, and that gives us the world upside down. Does you want to sleep there yourself, surrounded by the great economy of language? Scent around its delicate head seems good enough to eat. And now, having scoured the forest, will be losing more than this particular way. On whom go in and out revolving doors are hot on heels, the most flowery sweetness is ashamed of reason. From now on, tongue in the mud is a lover screaming for a serpent, or a window open to theatrical moonlight, or power-ground to pass the time, or a little nature tune about birds.

*

Suddenly we know swoony music fools us. Her eyes entwined around the command of seduction attend his needs while his mortal body opens. Honey-bags explode their calm rehearsal, as the point, so ripe with perfect timing, flies away like fate. Learn from your own misgivings what you can learn from the mistakes. Tricks about the natural world pile up accusations, he feels murdered by extravagant phrases of information. While he sleeps a million fail, swollen by the evening star.

*

A twinkle never chooses the simple route. To his feet the goddess spouts cherry lips, white hand. In this changeable dark manipulations reveal the building-up of person; magic, of course, is astonished. As you laugh notice the entire surroundings resound with your barking. Ghosts in their proper haunts turn the ocean gold. Entrances and exits keep track of real questions. He sees something: this spot at once recognizes what they might be doing here.

All That

He awoke with a pillow between sex and memory. He sat there, explained neither by substance nor dialectic. He found the red glow, touched a knob: in that second he was middle-aged. Hands outstretched, he began to retrace his steps.

Spirit should walk into that bedroom. In the beginning huge purposes had drawn him into romance, rub his temples through his reason, his tiny red beard. Trees—the young branch-like women and their ears—organs. His small eyes split in two.

He bowed his head with his hands, cafeterias, coffee. The details in which he dwelt subscribed to brochures. His father had come true in the usual way. He forgot why he could hear his own breathing.

The door opened: a bundle of clothes. He snorted, put on his pants, walked to the mirror. A former philosophic system prepared to take charge. We live forever.

Saturated

Up the ravine the sun was choking with dust. Emotion on the windows from the sideways heat, breathless their heads hang—they've stooped— and went in through the low doorway. On this dark corner table two glasses. His bold cheeks, his full lips—the ox. He was looking beneath the sunlight; every object was almost cool in the stream. Into his hands his pockets threw their coins.

I found a few words about each; nickname, unmarried, career, places in a mist of obscurity. In our part of the country, no one knew anyone, visited anyone, had money, noticed much. There were puzzling forces, inactive, having iron control. I have met no one else.

He played with his moods like a toy, climbed out of his skin. His gaze softened his lips into flourishes. He grew embarrassed and burst into laughter. All their eyes uncovered his face; far away began to fly into the room.

Like a trembling finger, the path lay across the field. At low tide I saw long wings oblivious of us. Everyone opened, as if silence was his . . .

Talking loudly, splutter up in the air and wave—they kept on repeating, "Come on, come on!"; his face was transfigured across the counter, summoned over to happiness.

I went out; the film of heat hung black over the blue sky. The grass had left behind no wind, against the windowpane wet hair was dancing. New faces had collected in the room. The sky was walking.

Sailed

Under a sky, in a garden, there are serious women and beautiful men, were talking. "You are much more beautiful," they implore, and can't help their red cheeks from flaming. "You are terrifying, too," and speak in the same voice.

He is already far away, is going to other trees on the horizon, disappear behind that cloud and drew around him closer a sleeping voice, lowered to a rolling feeling. In the dark she is sleeping, stroking on forever, buried in her hair this garden while the eyes of stupefaction widened, and the light curls lighting up this boy in the clouds would find him in some thick aureole covering her back and waking somewhere else . . .

I walk straight ahead, pays attention without always seeing, playing music the way I'd like to live. His lamentations would bring the cymbals together. I wanted to find out where they were enjoying themselves, followed them at a distance to where the beautiful nights dance like bears.

I've remembered a cup of brandy, and went to sleep turned toward their faces, the stars.

From the air there was his eye in his forehead, the sun had a brother. One of them said, "Yesterday moves so slowly." One of them said, "Seemed to linger with pleasure in the great hollow sky." One of them said, "Each setting out in solemnity from a beautiful night like this . . . "

Little Madrigal

I know nothing. These are things in themselves—obscure plaster; evacuation matter—the night at his feet of which the reporter was to interrogate.

I saw him coming and my heart beat so fast the metamorphosis was on the tip of my pen. Little madrigal—leaped up and said: "The entire outer world listens, weighed down by personal interest. But hotly, and proofs exist." He opened his door to embellishments and revealed himself better.

But shame, punishment, mercy make us leap to the skies—I kiss your hands plotting out the acts and scenes—all the submissiveness such a great fall requires. It makes me shudder, this peril, so drink to my health. The trouble with correspondence is more details.

Human Immune

I lie in your arms. I kiss your mouth. Use your nails, creature. Our roles— the crown, the infractions—inhabit this sanctified place to the point of fanaticism. I have to get my hands on the world.

Dead from complicity in San Francisco discharged me, the harp of a person had an arc. Then listen to inhale the contagion, where in the trap of your consciousness you have to pull to get out. Himself alone and scared kill mercies. The body has powers to paint yourself purple.

And shifting grasses, such erosion and mosses, nightjars lived on the drop-pings of sunny days . . . in that country of circumstances and moods—shattering its bark and throwing pieces of it around. Facing away from the entrance, with jerky movements kicking the sands backwards. I saw the size of a hand, losing hold of it . . .

Birdmen, across the rising hills and bay, rolling naked one night stirred and rose to the spell. He's out there, into the dead stumbling mind. I'll be accounting for no memory, without so much as a template. His nostril is hissing; his tongue in spasms. He has several parts on a breeze, an asylum this story surrounded. The face ripping wide open has led a team of men in white gowns and slow rhythm.

And twinges we ourselves devise woundingly by miscalculation—deli-cious conflagration winking—to become familiar and to pulverize them all. Curves could hope to find in this world no more beautiful hair. *Hell is round.* I squirted them with kisses. On his back at the edge of the couch to die of pleasure, kneeling into your asshole to form around me. Com-prise our friends the memory of the moments they passed in that virtue. Their honor therein, helpless before desire . . .

Where are you now, the harder you pull to get out? Then is that person fixing little sandwiches and watching TV? The Bay was fucked—ornate theories—there's the previous photo of "husband," hippies, Pt. Reyes beach, leering face, pink light, someone else. A portion of scripture, undi-agnosed. The placement of objects is a language theme, no longer private. A little old hairless man had swollen up. Pain is healing me into submis-sion, he wrote in his journal the secret of the universe: *hell is round.* You flop and thrash in fact.

The homecoming was marked and mapped; they circled in ever widen-ing loops. Processions migrating on blue nectar—stopping in the rising air over coastal waters. I waited I repeated I waited the test. The results were not fooled. I spent the summer as a natural landmark—the bearer of delicate organs—leaving the destiny dormant on dry days—moving my wooden ship to research, under spell of the spray. The sun was gigantic, slow, low-hanging. We had to acquire some knowledge in this year, food for a narrative. Summer is short. Inquiry raising our eyebrows was conta-gious. Moonlight on meat.

He knelt down next to me—fallen giant, empty stump. Feeling the blood pulling around my thighs, "I think it's screaming," I said. He stood barefoot, one warm leg, nest at the belt, pink wriggling sack, I wanted to run into the sun now, bristling muscular bulging animal sedated by his eyes. My body shook against him on a hot summer day, gushing to life, blood-filled, blood-dizzy. He rolled over onto his side, watching the men. A ruin. A patient. Overgrown so that the flat air had no answer. We floated in which the memory moving our bellies going dark have all taken flight—a cure may be possible—tell me what words mean—pleasure for a coffin: turn and enter your home.

The ghost which leads to burning incense on the altars of magical friends—these gods come upon gods which erects them—confections of the deific—showers down events, the smooth operations of insignificant romances to penetrate into their historian's hearts and foist upon the reader authenticity of the marvels . . . At last he dies, this exceptional man who loves them, phantom spawn, fraudulent cures, boundless poverty and the images of objects. Just a while ago I gave you attentions pure and simple. I take the oath worthy of your friendship exterminated in me. The lancing pain stuffing me with bucks and thwacks to distill soul's fuck: slip away, leave the rest to me, initiated into our mysteries . . .

With the Sixties the Seventies in Berkeley shot forward for replay to put the spaces where he wants—stars in the universe suggest metaphysical poets—lingered in remission studying the cosmic characteristics of T-cells. Triumphant skull in the grin of his malady, whacked as he was in a feedback loop. It's necessary to interpret men compared to sleepers in a private world. Two men pass through a forest which passed for the real world. From the cardiac ward through the underground corridor to encounter arrhythmia on the cathode screen. His head, his heart, a wave-form. And he spoke his monologue directed outward from the wisdom of a body: *hell is round*, the little clay pot locked up. The dream-time of heroes trying to throw up names: California, Parsifal, Chuck . . .

Night fell and a moon showed up between peaks. We were given a welcome for centuries. Aroused by smell in their human behavior a growl in heat, with a mixture of affection and respect. A little whipping, a little touching it lightly. One sometimes hears the ice snap with a seam in the center; large numbers breeding in our district at those breathing holes.

Members kill themselves, interested only in sugar. Suddenly the door was flung open, a youth tumbled in; the event we'd been preparing for changed our life entirely. To wake up to stop the alarm clock with one hand I lay on my right side facing my other—my Other Side—pressing the human places in a firm grip that woke us up in horizontal posture turned to face each other, covered with a thick blanket, the murmur of description, connected by an invisible rod as resistance fluttered back and forth.

The end of perspective, the proper shapes, blobs and pillars and singing minarets. You're a mess in the park. You're a willing dirty dog. With the sun disappearing a low fog tucked-up the air. I slept resting on the windowsill, stranger than birds. I used to be little but when we came back they were gone. Overnight to hear whatever was to be heard. With its overgrown boxed body jerking in perfect symmetry, this wizard—see what there is to see—bruised in deep breaths, and an archaeologist invited down to watch. He'd like to go from the bay to the ancient golden hills into the earth unannounced and never saying where. It was like some mechanical body secretly unstrung leaving accretions of soft dirt and mud. He kissed his waiting hand with both hands. The warm competence of the finished parts as if such machines had meaning. Touching it, the thin shell, tucked-in facing the bay may lie quiet in the dusk.

A way is opened; my initiated companions go after. Each gave his confrere the pleasure of sensations, sprawled on the stone floor. Sucking a moment of suspense into calm to savor its entirety, the combination of prick and ass and mouth, an eternity in that delirium he'll lie in your arms. Common measure in homage to fitting company. We'll make a circle *(hell is round)*, I want that energy while speaking, place yourselves close by me, excessive behavior swell discourse in proportion, the carnal prosperity of an everyday affair. It ripens and is born, having provided circumstances. Made an incision running around the head, then removed the strip of skin. Your body, the altar, on the altar. Go consult the children of love. There are minds, my friends, certain spirits, having rid themselves of vibrations, having progressed from extravagance to the speeding star, plagued in whose name passion alone dared multiply. Come—this'll serve as a bed—fuck my ass into my mouth.

This is what the dream referred to as *hell is round.* When he got out of the hospital it had the effect of wiping out history. Right now, the city was in intensive care, locked-out behind him. In the small room huge eyes flaming. His fried mind projecting on each side a sword to conquer—through the sense organs through the rain through the ward through the trembled fields of flowers as if shape had no substance through the living information completing itself. The blood of communion turning is a strange sentence. It broke through and fired experience at his head. Penetrated man penetrated himself. He was dragged through his address book deconstructed as official documents—the only way open. A limbo in lymphoma contemplated itself: he lived it, he loved himself, would love that too. He saw it spread out among us, pulled from his body. He could hardly wait to abolish himself, freeing him to go commando saving people, glommed onto another pretext in grief and love through the magical powers that underlay all his saved-up strategy . . .

I have variations about what was there: fathers, sons, and grandsons. When the sky cleared the weather superimposed corrections, noticing and recording more details. Fly to an elevated lookout post. It's my intention to describe history at the place we left them. Populations of flesh caught in our net. Of their courtship, of their species: their back was connected to display-movements fading toward the warm neck, a pirouette. Small circles this ceremony for hours on end. About the organization of behavior: some of them visited me. Animal behavior in the summer of 1956, or '76—embarrassing luxury—while we were floating on the shore or in the sea or under veils in quiet corners as the haze hanging behind us . . . Feverish outburst played havoc with their exact pose while sitting indoors, digging out of the morning for tests, returned positive results on the same day; distance . . . I've made a number of flights already—round flat discs—homing. Then my legs stopped moving altogether. Under the full microscope ferocity with nerve endings waiting I hovered, motionless, maneuvered into position.

I will see him standing, pounded, irresistible. In the dunes of my thick woolen sweater, dropped off along the western edge, panting through the indistinct sand, puncturing the middle of the farthest horizon, arms raised. Through the muscles of aching arms and legs opening on my back to the sea, wrapped in tangled sunlight staring beyond him. What

I didn't think or say fill my mouth, the terrible mysteries of sleep and navigation. We're best friends ever since ever. I noticed you in class—my full attention—if given the opportunity stammering to encompass love stanzas. Have you smiled?—choreography! Are you wrapped around my waist?—cosmic winds. San Francisco the beauty can take a picture—the air around him. I lay there on the floor, dug into the trenches, throwing down his trousers, the root of bones and mud and blood. I suppose he once lived here, curled into the tails of my nightshirt. He walked past me in his undershorts, an organism. We are the owner of sight and speech. In the gray light west of the Great Highway: not even me. We sat in silence, a blanket covering his lap. If you flew by you'd see these imposters, vapors of tenderness. It could never be contained.

Involuntary Lyrics: XXIV

the eyes
of cruising Dante named threading, stellar
compass to pass this way have done
with me or you, heart
warming literal your hands on me
held
sun
so art-
fully the
skill
employed rub down heat from on high art
hand lies
over heart
contain clamorous overbeating still

Involuntary Lyrics: LXXIII

a red lamp in the green of the night rest
head on his chest be hold
tight by him on fire

or hang
from neck as lie
like vertical weight off cold
toes warming day's breath expire
where he sang
through lungs by
breathing day
go or night come strong
in silence this west-
ern shore house bed with him on long
that trail away

Carol Snow

" . . . I am / what: an eye; attention? abstraction? / Null if I do not speak? This distance?"—"Prospect *(The Graces)*," quite the earliest of these poems. I remember that with the title's parenthetical I had hoped to invite other "Prospect" poems; and though no other pieces have been called such, distance and relation come so often into play here, the eye's continued concern with (questioning) its positioning.

Then self-awareness starts looping in and must be redirected outward, at least to the edge of itself and the world—that is, for one whose work would engage with experience as Matisse's engages with visual reality or Stravinsky's with consonance. . . . at least to the edge of itself and the world, an edge that language itself can refine and also complicate, compromise. "We are not allowing the whole of the bicycle / in here"— "Frame."

Then. Once certain personal difficulties had come manageably to light (in large part through writing), I wanted to allow for more of "the whole." To observe/include hearing, eventually, as well as sight, memory, event-objects—hearing, over which we have less control, which seems to bear some relation to compassion, and which of course has a peculiar intimacy with language and thought. "Bit" touches on this, on *syllable* and *sound.*

" . . . where 'then' was our seeing and moving closer . . . " And mean-

while. Ever. Expressive juxtaposition and investigative expression prove
fine pursuits: becoming art—I believe—only in love with 'the materials,'
in this case the music/imagery/play of language.

Prospect (The Graces)

At this distance,
space accumulates color—the luminous
blue of dusk acknowledging water, the water
a flatness so vast it seems to acquire height. And the mountains

bordering are without shadow or chiaroscuro—such black
solidity at this distance, I am
what: an eye; attention? abstraction?
Null if I do not speak? This distance?

*

Blackness against sea, against sky.
Mass refuting ascent, descent,
the feathered, the molten, the scattered;
against movement in water (the repeated breaking of surface).

Blackness

as solace so I waited
(as if I were distance) to give voice.
A blackness out of that privacy and silence we drown in.

*

Here are the Graces (this was said clearly):
Distance, Wash, Solidity—
the mountainous coast, black
and deafening or such that everything else fell silent.

Density, presence, stress—that Solidity;—
breath, not as wind and not rising and falling
pulled at weak edges like the sea,
but breath as a voice rising and falling.

[The Upward Is Endless]

The upward is endless.
     Sky, I mean: distance, rooted
among houses and trees, tangled in daylight
across a desk and down the inverted
spines of open books. And though gratitude sometimes
wells up, it is also like water in that it rises
upon itself . . .

     I watch a yellow chair—or rather,
watch the measurable distance to the chair—a little uncertain
even among belongings. The chill
on my skin is like fine silt, something failed
in rising but through which I move freely so it cannot be lifted.
           Maybe

 it is gratitude
I fear—the weight of it, flooding

into the external skeleton (this world
of things, I mean: bookshelves, rooms and window frames; fences, the
 branches and leaves of trees) and struggling

upward.

Positions of the Body VI

Wanting not only the stillness of hills,
but intercession—as by new grass

on the hills—with the silence
towering over the hills, Moore sculpts a massive

figure in black marble: a woman's
body, reclining, curved; eloquent

as bone, shell,
stones worn beyond contradiction.

*

You stopped
by the roadside, hills

lying in middle distance, few houses. Only the green
reaches of vineyard intervening

seemed manageable; that is, human—a matter
of scale; the silence was huge, so that only

the hills (which were huge,
also) could rest.

Cézanne, leaning to his canvas, would have mastered
that view, you thought: the blues and greens
and ochres of proximity and distance; that tenuous

position in the dance, not of the drawing
together of unlike, like bodies, but of the holding
apart of the body and terrain; you were held

so still, you thought that you might become those hills,
or must have been borne by hills,

or maybe your body
had been a maquette for the hills.

Frame

A composition is in the sliding mirror (so the edges of the world
weren't necessary after all!): with the vertical bar between window
    frames, then the cleft house and its neighbor
(but set in deep space)—framed, each behind a tree—fronted by a bird
    at the feeder
on the sill. *Outside.* A bright sky.
And glare, the reflected light from some pale siding in particular,
so that the series of birds feeding is a shadow repeating the shape of the
    (shadowed) figurine

on the sill—*in here*—but an animate shadow.
A print and a painting on the wall by the windows.

This much of a bicycle: foreshortened handlebars, a section of pitchfork
of frame, a shallow arc of wheel, a bike lock hanging from the
    handlebars
(all this upside down). I am hidden behind the file cabinet;
the bicycle is hanging from the ceiling but you will not know that.
We are not allowing the whole of the bicycle
in here.

Bridge

1) *IL MIGLIOR FABBRO*

And jumped up "to make tea," he said: an old man, having forgotten
rest—he couldn't "get flat enough"—kept lying down

and jumping up "to make tea"
(habit as the shell the husk the hull of mastery).

—Tension building in my shoulders aspiring to the grandeur of classical
    architecture (a Parthenon
or Temple of Athena Nike): noble but archaic—static, L. said—
the arch and the vault unknown.

—Changes in the flesh of a woman's body, described (as are hills' curves
by my drive over them to work) by instances over time of the motions of a
    bath towel over arms, shoulders, belly, breasts,
calves, thighs, crotch, buttocks, feet, in some usual order.

—A face only, wanting to emerge from water, making
a mask of the surface of the water, the surface
tension of the water unbroken
                     (is it an eye I mean? reflective and turning
    as toward prey—a man and two women standing at the railing of the
    Japanese footbridge
arched above and over the pond—
each thing seen, of the garden, shaken?)

And lapsed into silence, but a long silence.

*

As from no vantage.

From more than a darkness of eyes closed—
as from eyes closed in the darkness of a closed box.

Wanting the expression of no-face.
Not to speak not even to speak
tonelessly and without emphasis.

To go deeply into a flat dream of surface.

Water in the pond as that which has fallen (has found a level);
visages of garden, bridge, sky (supine and contingent—
collapsed on the skin of the surface) as its Heavenly firmament.

Flat. Flat! (Without affect.)

2) BRIDGE:

That I sat on a lawn between the houses—trees between the houses
unfamiliar, Eastern trees—between warm rains, alone

for a while, alone yet at ease as though 'in company': leaves
and the grass going on being green—or you could say

gods were there, " . . . Choros nympharum, goat-foot, with the pale foot
    alternate . . . "
                    That driving

to Chicago we stumbled through poems, shamefaced—nothing
of Crane between us and not much of Pound ("And . . . /And . . . " and
    "Choros nympharum . . . ") and fragments of Eliot,

words.
        'The real,' o my host—

that you also did laundry, you ended up driving, we sat on the bank of
    the river
at ease and 'in company.'

That since I came home I've been *vomiting memories. Clumsy.
'Stony.'

'Agony.'

*It fell apart there . .

                  (L., on the couch, had read "'Stony.' // 'Agony.'"
as irony, doggerel; I retreated
to the kitchen "to wash the dishes":
                  the world suddenly
flattened [around me, belongings detached and withdrawn, *no*—
    estranged, *no*—*disanimate* which had importuned me
for recognition; as from steps, rows of empty benches 'waiting,
    disconsolate'—*no*—on a concourse by a grove of trees at the park: I
    had seen they were flat
as ground, pebbles, etc.] so that I [—all the waiting
was mine] loomed up, with only the usual movements of my hands and
    the play

of water on the shine of the surfaces
buttressing me.
            Lines I had heard as "'Stony.' // 'Agony.'" extended,
    obliquely
toward—foolhardy
as prayer.

"If saying *is*
prayer?
Then *pray.*"
            —I'd thought something like that twice that day,
both times already safe, standing at the sink rinsing a washed plate
as I do [hands closed on opposite edges, rocking and rocking the surface
    under warm tapwater])

. . *where I couldn't say "lonely."*

3)

These things, flat: habit. Shadows.
Chance. The spare

face of the garden the garden
casts of itself across water; an uppermost layer

of pond water glazed with an outermost layer of foliage, bridge, trees,
   sky

(but art—the created thing:—rounded? slanted?
leaning?);
            a silence . . .

—The three had been talking, were leaning on the railing

of the Japanese bridge, the arc of the bridge
a darkness below them in the water.
                        Below them

leaves of nymphéas annexed the surface of the water, mimicked
the plane of the surface of the water, "supine
and contingent"; spread, flat in the second

world—the world
ceded, which shudders, is one layer—
                        but the leaves
interrupting! overlapping!

            These things,
upright: prospect; the greening of grass, of leaves,
in the primary. "Lonely" . . .

                        And the figures on the bridge
in the air, audacious

lilies—

Pool

Saw (into) and entered the wide corridor.
(Narrow room.)

Attracted by the promise of the purity of 'figure and ground.'

" . . . and the blue beside the white in the striping is the color / of the
    river Loire when you read about it in old books . . . ."

Yes, but that stripe or sash of white paper, a scroll
which turned corners—banding walls
'papered' with a brownish burlap—was wide, was water.

I have always adored the sea. And now . . .

                                    And painted blue
paper Matisse had *cut to the quick in color,* he called it, into the contours
    of portions
of bodies emerging from the—overlaid the—white; blue, whole
silhouettes arched like dolphins, expressing abandon—hovered,
    overlapping the—almost abandoning
the frieze, in places:

the frieze adorning the walls recreating Matisse's dining room.

Yes, but the doorways—so also a stretch of lintel
above which *Women and Monkeys* had hung—had been narrowed, so the
    area of the room was contracted.

As time is, in the Museum.

And now that I can no longer . . .

Walls recreating the walls of his dining room,
where Matisse worked on *The Swimming Pool* only in the evenings.

And time, in the work, is contracted.

I have always adored the sea, Matisse said. *And now that I can no longer go
    for a swim, I have surrounded myself with it.*

As white.

Yes, but noticed in one corner an area of white for which blue forms
    served—not as bodies—as borders but open: walls of a corridor or
    banks to a channel
of white, the white itself—'broad' would be a pun—pooled,
    recognizably
bodily; and then—

where 'then' was our seeing and moving closer to see more closely—

                                                                a passage
where fragments of blue (but almost body almost) fragmented the white
    so that
neither color was 'figure' or 'ground'—emblem, banner—anymore, yet.

Bit

'A slight'

sounded.

Reverberating—in what box?—or reiterated
—like a booster shot, like the roosters in Bishop—sustained

(this illustrated by my tilting half a glass of orange juice
up over an empty glass—"I'm a little teapot . . . ";
more precisely: The Mystery Spot, "Cannons ready!" horizon to the rim,
    the extreme verge,
surface tension [J. knew a word for it]—pouring
[not spilling, by virtue of the empty glass, not threatened]
suspended), suspended.

One survived—a part of her part of a part of the story
replaying in excerpts in the Holocaust Museum—the forced, then called
    a Death,
March through the dead of winter among thousands, among hundreds,
    by spring, tens,
of three young women struggling abreast, arms linked so that in turn,

the one in the middle could sleep. 'The whole for a part'

then 'a part for the whole,' her visage, *a certain Slant of,*
quote, what a bell
meant (the sound of [J. would know the word]—'synecdoche'), *so one of*
us could sleep.

Heard (as thought)
but also spelled (?!): 'a slight'

—not yet insult, minor, a slip of a

Susan Stewart

How I Wrote My Poems

Although I write individual poems without deciding, as I begin, the forms they might take or the direction of thought they might pursue, I do eventually create a particular frame that will inform each book. After I have a sense of this frame, I start to write toward it and revise heavily as I go along, letting fairly long periods of time pass before I feel I'm finished with any given poem. And then I try to think about what the frame is resisting or addressing and use those insights to revise again. Working this way makes me one of the slowest poets.

The Forest was concerned with the relations between unconscious and conscious knowledge of the past. I finished a draft of it in the early 1990s and then I was dissatisfied with it formally and started over again. I wanted to find ways to make time a material part of the book itself, so I invented forms with that goal in mind, as in "The Arbor," where the original poem goes down the left side and the right side is a later gloss on its meanings. Some poems are repeated and reappear with new material, others move backward in time to a point of origin.

From the mid-90s on, I worked on the poems of *Columbarium* as what I called a "shadow georgic." I knew I would write the major part of the book as an alphabet so that I could evoke memory practices, though I decided to write a number of poems for each letter to avoid the tedium of

From an interview with Jon Thompson in *Free Verse*, Spring 2003.

a one-to-one structure throughout. I was still preoccupied with the relations between knowing and not knowing, which I think of as a dynamic of poetic composition more generally. But now I wanted to turn toward the future and use the georgic form, since georgics traditionally involved the transmission of knowledge from a member of one generation to a member or members of another. The problem I faced was finding ways of avoiding the didacticism of the georgic, so I saw the notion of "shadow," or the underside of knowledge and the unforeseen consequences of knowledge and technology, as a useful metaphor. Then working . . . on *The Elements*, I explored the forces of nature that are a threat to georgic transmission. I gave the book a structure that moves from unintelligibility to intelligibility and back again—there is a nest of georgics at the center of the whirling forms of the works on the elements.

*

Poetry—in its making and reception bound up with the somatic, with memory as well as sense experience, and with the overdetermination of symbols—opens to new knowledge because it is not bound by received habits of perception and understanding and, because, like all art, its aims are non-teleological.

Error is inevitable, it seems, in both ethical and aesthetic judgments, but the consequences are not the same. In making poems, writing critically, and teaching I have the freedom to see error as a blessing, for error is a mark of departure from perceptual and cognitive habits. I don't think there can be errors of imagery or rhythm or voice, for example, so long as the intention to make the poem has not been crippled by external or conventional demands. Scholarship can take a wrong direction or be blighted by errors of fact, but to create new knowledge scholars also have to be willing to go beyond the usual frames for thinking. While most of life presses finite requirements upon us, creative and critical work has the luxury of being an incomplete project. I'd find reality, the reality of history, unbearable without the openings offered by works of art.

Medusa Anthology

1

Now my God in your firmament,
now the stars turn, inhuman, above
the grasses. Show me your face
in ice, in pond, in shop glass.
Out of the vacuum spun from
your boredom, and the humming,
electric, beneath the asphalt ground,
keep us from harm and breaking.

2

Now the stars turn, inhuman, above
the grasses and the filament
fades to red, going out.
Will you touch us again
with what you made and
then unmade? Undone;
still, stillness. Send us
the starry, far-seen, sign.

3

Show me your face there in ice,
in pond, and shop glass.
Beak to beak, claw to claw,
they hovered and dropped,
but only one flew away
to the lamppost: hold the mirror
steady and turn the fierceness back
to the eye from whence it came.

4

Sacks, bags, vents, packs, something;
someone's someone, outside the opera—O,
spare something, something to eat, want,

nothing, no change, have no change,
nothing now, nothing on me.
Thou munna' wan', munna' wan'
must not, must not, must—
have no change on me.

5

The only politic lies in particularity,
lies in gutter, gutted, or on the grate.
The grate rusted, warm, cold;
the cold, blue blanket, moth-
gnawed world, cobbled together on the re-
production cobblestones. (Lamp-
light, star-light, good-night,
ladies, goodly-night, 'night.)

6

Show me your face in ice and glass.
There was an enormous, dark, and many-
figured painting that appeared
when a plague cursed the city and
its kings. And we heard
a broken voice tell the story of a ship-
wreck, stuttering, "Wha-wha
what is Hecuba to me?"

7

A blanket of blue acrylic, not like
the functions and forms of conceit.
"It was an embarrassment to the monarchy
that the government frigate *La Méduse*
was lost in 1816. The passengers
were abandoned by the crew on a make-
shift raft on which nearly all
perished." Perish, the thought, memory now

8

Receded. The history soonest forgotten.
"The masts and beams had been crudely lashed
together with ropes and belts and winches."
"Steering an erratic course off the coast
of Senegal." Let us draw our attention
to the adverb, to the precise quality
of action with which the thing is done-
and let us become the enemies of style.

9

Nothing but, or in, particularity.
The task of history as a cliché
about forgetting. Steering an erratic course,
on a makeshift raft on which nearly
all perished. Herded onto the slippery
beams, one hundred and fifty people
slipping, spilling, at once,
the raft unbalanced by the weight.

10

I will gladly pay you a nickel today
for an enormous, dark, and terrible canvas
on which you will represent yourself to me
and others who should like to know you
better. "It sunk three feet
immediately and the people were shoved
and huddled together so tightly none
could move or cry out."

11

The great roof fretted with gold,
the goodly frame bereft of terror
and fear—where were you when they
bundled the poor one away,
her brown coat, her matted hair,

collapsed on the curb: rain,
red tip, ginkgo budding out,
that day, the fire/medic truck

12

Blurting and wailing in flash and flash again?
Among the survivors was a woman
who wrote an unbearable story, telling how
they had promised to stay with
the raft and, together, pull it
to a nearby shore,
but the men in the boats soon cut
the cables, leaving the crew

13

To the currents and the winds, and the battering
noise of the waves.
In the night the sea rose and carried
many away and drowned the ones,
too, who could not move their limbs.
"The second night whoever could not
reach the center perished, often
stifled by the weight of his comrades."

14

Nothing pays that kind of money,
except, maybe, playing the numbers.
One of them is spending most of his time
trying to keep the clients on the welfare rolls;
still, the restaurant filled up before we noticed
and the atmosphere became, like, festive.
The hard ones always sing for their supper,
but a little Lord's Prayer wouldn't hurt.

15

Wait now boy, don't you cross
that street. 'Nice wedder dis

mawnin' sezee. Hopefully,
like really, he held
up his shield, stopping
the traffic in its tracks.
Some said the only cure for a stutter
was to sleep with a penny beneath your tongue.

16

O, what a rogue and peasant
slave are you. And is it not monstrous
that the function seems to serve
what is known of the forms of conceit?
Hector was the best and the dearest
of her sons, for he fired the ships
without a thought or hesitation.
By your smile, you seem to say so.

17

Say, sir, spare something, sir?
Be of service, sir, spare, something?
Spare service, sir, be something,
something spare and serviced,
sir, say something, something, sir,
say, spare sir, be spare
sir something, sir spare something,
be, say, sir, something, spare.

18

Wha-what is He-Hecuba to me?
Death had saved us from the waves
in the night, but the soldiers
and sailors drank themselves sense-
less. On the third day raging
hunger overtook the weakest wills
and some turned to the corpses for
their bread and meat and drink.

19

"Those whom death had spared, in the disastrous
night of wave and wind, threw
themselves ravenously on the dead,
with which the raft was covered,
cut them up in slices which
some even that instant devoured.
A great number of us at first
refused to touch the horrible food.

20

But at last yielding to a want
still more pressing than that of humanity,
we saw in this frightful repast
only deplorable means of prolonging existence.
Those who abstained were granted more wine.
But from the fourth day on, all
practiced cannibalism, supplementing
their ration of wine with seawater and urine."

21

On the sixth day, most, covered
with large wounds, had wholly lost
their reason. It was decided
to throw the sick into the sea.
When the *Argus* came, seven days
later, fifteen were left and
five died on shore. O, bright-
eyed looker in the peacock's tail,

22

What did you see beyond the
erasure? We shed "tears of blood,"
we "averted our eyes," we threw
the swords and sabres to
the waves—for they inspired us with

a horror that we could hardly conquer
as we pulled our faces tightly against
the scene of salt, and wreck, and drying blood.

23

What did you hear and not hear
in the night, was the moaning
the inverse of all this certainty
of number? For a witness can surely count,
remembering the look on a face, long before
the story is stitched by causality
and blame. Goodly night fretted
by fear, a story lashed together

24

By means of masts and sodden timbers.
How infinite in faculty, how like
a dream of passion, how like a painting hanging
so strangely out of fashion. Cassandra was raped
beside the altar, and Paris foiled, and Troilus
altered by love in unseemly, untimely, dress.
Why not, why not, why not, why not tender
tenderness, thus tendering something still?

25

What's Hecuba to him or he to Hecuba that he . . .
They bundled her into the fire/medic truck
while the dispatcher blurted
addresses and numbers, stuttering
blur so urgent and erratic.
During the curfew the homeless
lived beneath the trees and the soldiers
grew confused by their leafy camouflage.

26

That day, rain, ginkgo budding out,
spare something for someone to

eat. "That from her working all
his visage wan'd." And she remembered
the best and dearest of her sons
who, too, had been a coward,
strutting and bragging. When they left,
the print of their boots remained

27

And the dry space where her body had been.
A sweeter child there never was,
the sweetest flower of all our youth and still
not yet employed. And from his working
all her visage waned, and turned stone
cold while the rain erased her shape-
less, hapless shadow. Some
avert their eyes, some shed reddish tears.

28

It became the official policy
that on the first day of May, nineteen
ninety-two, all the boats would be turned
back, regardless of circumstance.
Day after day they studied
the sun, until the knowledge
of fire drew them headlong into
blackness, the blind spot hovering

29

Just above the waterline, drew
them the way a thread is drawn through
a needle, along a slight arch,
and then caught. *Ki sa*
u fè, ki sa w'ap-fè,
y-ava-neye-l,
mi wi tel im di
truut, di verité.

30

Show us your face, Lord,
like a spot on the sun
and we'll remember
how that black shape was
a projection from
our long-spent longing
for a starry sign
against our delirium.

31

Keep us from harm and breaking,
turn the eye from whence it came.
What are you doing
and what have you done?
They'll drown him, yet I
must tell them the truth—
how the beggar sleeps
beside the palace of music,

32

How the raft was set adrift from
its erratic course, how the woman
collapsed below the high window,
how the city burned and the boats
were turned away. How plain is
our faculty beside thy wrath
and thy will which thou hast
done. What can we see beyond

33

The erasure? Eyes to see, ears
to hear. Tongues to tell the difference
between syllable, tear, and pattering rain.
In action Cassandra was like an angel;
in apprehension, like a god herself,

but the words she spoke
mi wi tel im di truut
were all for nothing or less.

34

History soonest forgotten,
the starry far-seen sign still
send us. Touch us again
with what you unmade,
then made, slowly flame
the wire we've hung here,
figure a line between
the throw of sparks.

35

Cursed boat, and plague, and port,
tangled limbs between the planks,
sterile outcrop of the dead—
goodly frame bereft of theme,
crabbed notations in a book.
Keep the book from harm and breaking,
wake us now from awful sleep,
show us thy stone, thy stone made flesh.

The Seasons

Ice-jammed hard-clasped branches in the blocks a whole river of them
yet at the same time, the time sensed
beneath the time walked, the time breathing in and out, the water almost
eddying, still pushing there beneath
the milk-white surface, deep down and over the bed of rocks; you could call
them frozen, though they never live
another state than less and less until they're gone, the water going on and on
until it all accrues again. The seasons
always seemed to be a form of freedom, something good for making meaning,
the kind of notion a founding father could

pull out now and then whenever
the now and then would flag. Time
healing time, you know the saw.
Lightning strikes and struck.
The shepherd fell down dead.
And then it all wound up again: a redbreast made a ruckus, the quick
    eternal sprung.
You wanted summer or you wanted death.
So death came again, and that was autumn.

Wrought from the generation of EARTH

One boot planted, firm as a trunk, the other shoved down on the shovel,
shoving with a human weight that barely dents the crust
over the outcrop of flinty veins that plumb through clay and chalk.
Struck down bluntly over and over, the shovel bounces back,
ringing the facts. Even the dead must wait above ground
for a hard winter to thaw. Nothing to do but wait, hoping for
the ground to give, hoping the corpse won't wander.
Freezing up, the bulb cracks, aborting its bloom, and the smaller
half falls away—all things bearing their own teleology,
all things turning out or not—the husk shrivels back across
the pod and the young mice lie stiff in their nest. Coming to be
collapses, radiant as a berry trapped in ice.

Under the dazzle of the white light on the whiteness, only
the forms remain, a solid geometry slumping at its edges;
you can't tell the difference between a rock and a hard place, or a sled
and a wheel-barrow sunk into the compost. The tar caddies
steam on every block, buckets of hell-sludge go up single file, plugging
the gaping roots, or are passed down to craters where traffic
ruts and wheels are wrenched away. A tomb is pried up, then resealed.
Skull-duggery, boneyards, dustbins. The endless digging and patching
of the world. A new wound is cut, then healed.
The dew evaporates from the softening snow; you can see your breath

and know you are breathing and that is enough to make you want to speak
in the season of longest nights.

The frail root stirs, a shiver runs down the hinges of the night-crawler, a slight
quiver ruffles across the hunched neck of the wren. One day a breeze arrives,
and her winter wings shake free with each short hop to the seed after next.
It doesn't take a crowbar when the door is open. Mud turns to muck,
the blood begins to thin, the rusted joints are oiled and move again.
The ice breaks and jams the river, sounding like distant guns, while the pitch-
fork goes in and out with ease. What will come back comes back and what
doesn't come back stays, too, somehow nascent or caught within the bramble,
slowly losing its name and form.

The broom sweeps up and wears away, sweeping itself into a stump. Pebble
tags weed and weed tags clod—fatigue of the soiled world, fatigue-dragging
shoe, dragging shoulder and fist, the effort toward consequence, clenched and
released in rhythm. Crops fail or flourish, toys of the weather, and the weather
does not think of us in turn. Spirit who needs a look-out, spirit not in our
image, he drops to the horizon, gathering speed. The absolute form of offering
repeated, the absolute form of earthly repetition, churning and churning
along the furrow.

There by the side of the churning sea, the plowman's bent doubled in the field,
sees a dark fleck
—no, white wings—moving toward the sun,
but does not see his fall, or even dream a man
could free himself from ground
and somehow fly.

Work is wrenched from the thick, from the dense, from the places where
resistance is clotted with stones. The rake gets tangled with sticks and vines,
the scythe chips off and leaves a ragged swathe.
Mud muddies the spring and can only be settled by gravity. The sun takes aim
at the nape of the neck, the crown, or right between the eyes.
Spoiled saints listen for miracles while the cooks sift pebbles from the grain.

What is primitive in memory stays buried in memory. Things made of earth
sink deeper into earth and begin to be earth again: a vase blown from sand

and fire; the clay lamp shaped by a hand long dead and water long ago drawn
back into its bed; a spoon thinned into a silver lattice soon to be flecks
of silver again. Deep in the mine, fire flames from the methane
or shines for no reason from the diamond's splinter.

Dust rolls cells and crumbs and lint and binds them loose with hair.
Amber hardens around the spider, the bones melt into the peat.
The soil lies opened to the gaze of the heavens like a memory exposed to light.
Vase, clay lamp, and silver spoon, working loose, come glinting as shards
to the surface.

Went down to the shore where the beach was hard,
went right to the edge of the inhabited world,
built a ditch and a castle, a minaret, a draw-bridge,
shaping heads and limbs from the sugary sand.
Then fast-flung, crashed, a single wave
erasing, though every grain of sand remains.

This was the only world, the world where we awakened, where the sky gods
hold one handle of the plow and the gods of the dead hold the other.
The brown gods rose from the mud and the ponds, and crept along the paths
and had no names. And then the gods concealed in gypsum fought against
the fathers, rising up in fury, inconsolable. When the wars of heaven ended,
sky held dominion, dominion over all below.

Deep where the bloodless ghosts assemble, at the still base of the revolving
world, the girl sorted seeds in the lap of her apron, letting each one count
as a month, letting three count as a season, saying six will count as
the darkness and six will count as the light. She sang to herself,
sang the whole day through, knotting rings and necklaces
from coarsest blades of grass. She sang a walking song
and dreamed, her corduroy blanket abandoned to fray and
lint for the birds to weave.

Look for her, lie along the meadow; you can hear the hum
of the stalks and leaves, the full buzz so unlike
a shell's hollow roar. Lie along the field and feel the mineral cold,

bone-chilling deep below the warmth of the loam. Lie in the dead leaves
and do not make a sound and love will cut furrows in the soil of grief.

This was the only world: great scar, worn away by reverence and harm.
Permanence out of which all things that perish rise; permanence in which
each enduring thing will perish. Not the earth surrendered or asunder.
Not the earth itself, but tenderness.

Cole Swensen

Poetry allows us to throw into question precisely what daily living forces us to accept as given—language, and thus all that it constructs. Which some argue is everything. At the very minimum, poetry allows us to question (as in "to interrogate" as well as in "to doubt") meaning and sense, their relationship and their limits.

The very point where sense begins to break down is also where it begins to open out, and I find that I'm often trying to get right to that point and then project a little beyond. Daily language comprises a stable field of communally agreed-upon sense, but out toward its edges, when language is used in unusual ways, that stable field begins to break up; it gets fissured through with gaps where no sense, or non-sense, takes its place.

During most of our lives, we simply ignore the gaps in sense, but poetry can use language in a way that brings them to our attention. And once they've come to our attention, we start to notice that new things, new kinds of sense, accrete in them. These points of breakdown, these gaps, are not found just by art—they're also found by violence and war, by love, wonder, and fear—by any experience that takes us to the unique. But I think the arts are particularly able to mold new accretions in constructive ways.

Some of my recent work is related to visual art because it seems that the visual arts have a completely different and often more available avenue beyond the territory of established sense. In querying paintings, I'm trying to follow them beyond language, where they have a surer footing.

And what is the point in pursuing beyond sense? There are two, I believe. One is that sense simply does break down; we do find ourselves beyond it, and often it's dangerous and frightening. We need to know how to negotiate this zone, and how to transform it in cases of war and fear and grief into something that won't simply overwhelm and destroy us.

And the other point is to isolate and present beauty, which resides almost exclusively beyond the limits of sense. I believe in beauty, in its possibility, but also in its complexity—that it fissures through terror and violence, too; that it comes mixed into myriad human situations. Isolating the strand of beauty in situations that are otherwise negative can offer a way to address them.

I also think we perceive much more beauty than we can articulate—yet the attempt to articulate it brings beauty in closer, allows us to incorporate it and then use it as a bridge to yet more subtle beauties.

Whenever language deviates very far from the daily through manipulations of syntax, sentence structure, word choice, and other staples of much contemporary poetry, we find ourselves beyond sense, which can be empty or dissatisfying. Its pleasures seem more available when experienced in contrast to sense, so I try to keep one foot (to go back to the field analogy) on firm ground, while the other wanders outward. Often that firm ground is readily recognizable sense itself, but at times I try to use sound relationships to hold together what might not otherwise cohere.

I think, too, that music has a sense of its own, and though it can't be articulated, some part of our psyche nonetheless recognizes that sense and is comforted by it. I'm hoping that that musical comfort and pleasure will overflow into and assuage any linguistic discomfort, making readers more at ease with forays beyond normative language use.

Like many people working today, I'm particularly interested in connections and relationships—at times more than in the things they bring together. This is in part because the gap a relationship spans is often analogous to the gaps that open up at the limits of familiar sense, and in part because in relationships, one finds a vital motion and the perspective from which "things" cease to be things because they are no longer static or finite, but are always changing according to context. It's a perspective in which things reveal themselves to be, like Wittgenstein's words, determined only by use.

Perhaps I'm concentrating on this recently because I find myself increasingly drawn to *things*, to the material aspects of the world, in my work. Does poetry try to reflect the world in some kind of clarifying way, or does it try to construct an alternative world so close that we won't notice the substitution? I'm not sure, but I'm more interested in the former, which is what has increased my interest in history over the past several years. The world is never just what's here on a given day, but is all the days before as well, and they constitute additional places where we can and do live. I don't think an understanding of history will aid us in the present or anything like that, but I do think it extends the world in a very real way—just as extending the territory of sense extends the world. Perhaps the most basic project of sentient beings is to grow the world.

January

The green sea carves up the sky

Origami folds of the fortune-telling square small hands
who could have known. The sun storm remote

weather high water on the beach the burning calendars

Cattle sparkling. Gray hills a layered near
"This is the church and this is the steeple"

Had thought. And then must be believed:
The green sea the aided flight (we were flying

when you woke up and screamed

Beauty entirely color. It is winter and that
burns slowly

Histories

To what
people say. Wide alley of elms. This
architecture the body cannot

If each word were to be replaced by gesture

Sculpture like the wind takes forever. Decades
in themselves no mark on

Trace those rivers on the globe the tip of a finger

The warrior-herdsmen stand with their ankles crossed
to indicate

(Oh love of sun (are we still falling. A letter
its stamp and you try to match

I watch through the window across the street a man
a book there on the table open a fragment

overheard conversation or you stand in the crowded room,
nothing in your hands way over there

The Landscape Around Viarmes

1

There is someone here who looks like you. Face after face across this expanse. Extend and turn. If you turned around you'd be facing a forest. There is someone (If I turned around) (I should say "If" and then "I"). The face is by definition something turning. (Everywhere you turn you see the face of God). (Koran Chapter 2 Verse 115). There is someone looking through a magnifying glass at his hands.

2

And there is someone there blind as the sky. Birds going crazy in the rising heat. Heat rises. The human body falls at 32 feet per second. The human body falls. There are many of us here. Turn around. Turn your face to the wall. The forest in the Middle Ages ran from here to the Baltic Sea. Continuously. These bodies appear inside their skins. There is something facing. There is no one looking. There is someone here. Right here.

3

Landscape is light alone. Some white coming up from behind which like a pendulum will come to entrance. To evoke along. The border of a lake bordering the face. There was no one there. That turns and one after one. It is the repetition that makes it concrete. That makes it fall. The human body is blind except for the minute exception of the eyes. The variable sky extends inside. It is that gasp across which in turning you catch a glimpse. Five million trees. We are barely alive.

4

Chapter 2 Verse 115. Everywhere you turn you see I met a child in the forest. His hands were broken and broken things were in them and he smiled. Water water burning bright. We were all there and we all turned at the sound and there was no one there. If we repeat it often enough it will. Repeat after me "The human body falls" and the landscape thus becomes. You can live. A somewhere here and then you turn. We'll all be there and we'll all wave and blow a kiss and then wave again.

5

If you stop the sound of water will not. And the child turns blurring the image at the edges. There is a forest. Continue. It has no border. Repeat. When the water stops and we were all there and speechless. There is a moment as the charge is changing poles that a perfect balance is struck and a pause. Pause. Now resume. The child must walk alone from here to the Baltic. Turn around slowly. Look at me speechless without speaking.

6

And there. There is water stretching farther in which no face and on with the multiplicitous body. The one after one after one. And the tender part that lines the inside of the arm. If you follow the vein with your tongue. Stop. The multiplication of trees and the perfectly symmetrical features of the face. It was not your face and you turned Chapter 2. The child in a blur in your hands which are repeated past recognition. Small and identical birds.

7

And in this one a landscape that begins. Refuse. And it rolls on and sometimes changing direction or tone until it turns and the face of God divides the body into millions. Trees and all their hands repeating some gesture as a grammar of ungraphable space. From here to the sea a single child with separate hands that spread unchecked that fly close to the ground that wind and unwind that you saw and mistook once before.

8

Trace the grain. The forest that couldn't follow that finds within nonetheless the face cannot be repeated even if the eyes. Mile after mile sea after child. One with glass hands and all of us still. And it grows against while yet within you and because of what will and what does. We did. All of us ready and the light leaving the body in droves. We were standing and slightly startled. The burnished silence and unable to move.

9

And it wasn't you. There the forest breaks down and no longer. God has a face. We can't be seen. Verse 115. The proximity glides. There is someone and there is something and often in the forest alone and it slides. Repeat. It practically lives. Repeat. I remember only the parts that begin. The field opens onto. And in the evening thousands but they were birds and they fell through the sky sideways.

The Invention of Streetlights

> *noctes illustratas*
> (the night has houses)
> and the shadow of the fabulous
> broken into handfuls—these
> can be placed at regular intervals,
> candles
> walking down streets at times eclipsed by trees.

*

Certain cells, it's said, can generate light on their own.

There are organisms that could fit on the head of a pin
and light entire rooms.

Throughout the Middle Ages, you could hire a man
on any corner with a torch to light you home

                                    were lamps made of horn
and from above a loom of moving flares, we watched
Notre Dame seem small.
Now the streets stand still.

By 1890, it took a pound of powdered magnesium
to photograph a midnight ball.

*

While as early as 50 BCE, riotous soldiers leaving a Roman bath
sliced through the ropes that hung the lamps from tree to tree
                    and aloft us this
                    new and larger room
Flambeaux the arboreal
                was the life of Julius Caesar
    in whose streets
    in which a single step could be heard.
We opened all our windows
and looked out on a listening world laced here and there with points of
   light,
                  Notre Dame of the Unfinished Sky,
oil slicks burning on the river; someone down on the corner
striking a match to read by.

*

Some claim Paris was the first modern city to light its streets.
      The inhabitants were ordered
        in 1524 to place a taper in every window in the dark there were
           912 streets

walked into this arc until by stars
makes steps sharp, you are
and are not alone
by public decree
October 1558: the lanterns were similar to those used in mines:
"Once
we were kings"
and down into the spiral of our riches
still reign: *falots* or great vases of pitch lit
at the crossroads
—and thus were we followed
through a city of thieves—which,
but a few weeks later, were replaced by chandeliers.

*

While others claim all London was alight by 1414.
In utter vigil ordered:
Out of every window, come a wrist with a lanthorn
and were told
hold it there
and be on time
and not before
and watched below
the faces lit, and watched the faces pass.   And turned back in
(the face goes on) and watched the lights go out.
Here the numbers are instructive:
In the early 18th century, London hung some 15,000 lamps.
And now we find (1786) they've turned to crystal, placed precisely,
and each its own distance, small in islands, large in the time it would
take to run.

*

And Venice started in 1687 with a bell

upon the hearing of which, we all in unison

exit,

match in hand, and together strike them against an upper tooth and
touch the tiny flame to anything, and when times get rough (crime
up, etc.) all we have to do is throw oil out upon the canals to make
the lighting uncommonly extensive. Sometimes we do it just to shock
the rest of Europe, and at other times because we like it.

*

Says Libanius
       Night differs us
              Without us
              noctes illustratas
    Though in times of public grief
when the streets were left unlit, on we went, just
dark marks in the markets and voices in the cafes, in the crowded
squares,
a single touch, the living, a lantern
     swinging above the door any time a child is born, be it
Antioch, Syria, or Edessa—
and then there were the festivals,
            the *festum encaeniorum,* and others in which
            they call idolatrous, these torches
                   half a city wide
                     be your houses.

The Hand as Historical

A fossil hides time—and thus from itself, that else

is the human compass

is the hand—and owns

composite home, its only hour, and that, in fact, the graph
is a palm—just look what falls within

       (which lands, is said, which knows its way) was day
       before the latter was invented—all is lost

is said: what spine is this? or better put, what animal
with five spines (Who survived?) A fossil is a photograph of chance.

The Bones of the Wrist

Scaphoid=boat-shaped; Unciform, a hook; a half-moon, a wedge, a pea,
and no longer parallel, all combine to wrist. Paved from there to the sea,
all the stones spin. And wouldn't you find the click into another piece of
thought, one just to the left as the ocean slips and the hand reaches out to
calm the trembling man.

Windows in Paintings

Because a window is always relative to a body, and the body is never re-
peated. Thus proliferates. Because every body involves a window or win-
dows. The number of body parts out there in the world "at large," as they
say, the body is not single. And though painting was invented to correct
this, it has ended up accomplishing the opposite. Errant the eye. And the
mode of traveling based on forgetting, that we also labeled 'body' so that
these windows bring us back, but not to us.

Versailles of the Scattered Here

Statues are a way for a king to be
    everywhere at once the body flung. There was
a time it rained gloves; another time, hands.
    They hold on. A king will turn
into history, and this is what it is to have a body
built of snow—lungs of snow and eyes and ice. From time to time,
Louis XIV placed living men dressed as stone
    among his guests who would then burst forth,
as if he himself, my twenty fingers, he said, my seventy, I am.

Of the Insistent Equation of Opposites

You build a garden just like you build a fortress—to see the future.
It's what you see there
that changes
        the entire landscape
                into the world
                      we remember
or the shadows of yews
            cut into cones
become swords in the late afternoon
lying flat across a lawn so interminably lost. A garden is a war
that cost a war.
        And so it was there
               after all
that it took place (which is to say, the place was taken
away.

Rosmarie Waldrop

Why Prose Poems?

I love the way verse refuses to fill up all of the available space of the page, so that each line acknowledges what is *not*. And I love the way poetry's rhythm, maybe its very essence, arises from the tension, the mismatch between line and sentence, between the halt at the "turn" that interrupts the syntactic connection and the meaning's push forward toward completing the sentence.

For the fraction of a moment, this void stops everything. It suspends the assurance of statement to reintroduce uncertainty, possibility, potential. According to Hölderlin, the gap of the caesura, metrical poetry's additional locus of disjunction, blocks the hypnotic enchantment of rhythm and images: to make us aware of representation itself. Or, as I would say: of language itself. Or of the silence that makes possible the music.

I have pursued this void, this numinous showing of language. I tried to exacerbate the tension and disjunction between sentence and line by keeping the lines very short while opening the confines of the sentence into one quasi-unending flow.

> *In order not to*
> *disperse*
> *I think each movement of*
> *my hand*
> *turns*
> *the page*
> *the interval has all the rights*

But I began to long for complex sentences, for the possibility of digression, for space. The space of a different, less linear movement: a dance of syntax. The prose paragraph seemed the right kind of space where form could prove "a center around which, not a box within which" (Ezra Pound).

I gave up stress for distress (as Charles Bernstein likes to say), the distress of lacking coordinates, of the unstructured space of prose, the uncharted territory of the page. The excitement and terror of the open. Versus the challenge of closure: in the complete sentence and, extreme, in the proposition. But no. This was not enough tension. Not enough to compensate for the absence of *turning,* of margin. I must try to move the vacancy and the mismatch from the margin inwards.

   the empty space I place at the center of each poem to allow penetration

I must cultivate cuts, discontinuities, ruptures, cracks, fissures, holes, hitches, snags, leaps, shifts of reference, and emptiness *inside* the semantic dimension. *Inside* the sentence. Explode its snakelike beauty of movement. A different kind of speed. An energy that knots and unknots constellations before they can freeze into a map.

"Gap gardening," I have called it, which is just another way of talking about poetry as concentrated language. Making dense, cutting out steps. My main tool is collage, which brings with it displacement and dialogue, makes audible that we always write on a palimpsest. Though what matters most to me while composing is the cut, the fragmentary, "torn" nature of the elements, and the spark given off by the edges.

But what has become of sound? When "free verse" took a step away from meter, it was a step away from the oral. The prose poem moves yet farther in this direction. Its sound and rhythm are subtler, less immediate, less "memorable." If it counts, it counts words or sentences rather than stresses or syllables. Valéry's definition of the poem as "a prolonged hesitation between sound and sense" does not work here. The fissure is now more between sense and sense, sense and syntax, density and intensity.

But there are many kinds of music. Syntax is rhythm, sound in motion. Even if sound does not seem to be in the foreground, it is the body, the materiality of poem. What carries the surface we call mind. It is (mostly) the sound that short-circuits the word's transparency for the signified, which some consider its advantage. "A symbol which interests us also as an object is distracting," said Susanne Langer. This "distraction" is exactly what I want, what poetry worth the name gives us: a word that does not disappear into its meaning, a word-thing, palpable, a sensuous, sounding body. The word made flesh. The flesh of a bird, so it can also take wing. Toward the kind of mathematic limit where, to vary Zukofsky, the word approaches both the wordless art of music and the soundless music of silence.

Feverish Propositions

You told me, if something is not used it is meaningless, and took my temperature, which I had thought to save for a more difficult day. In the mirror, every night, the same face, a bit more threadbare, a dress worn too long. The moon was out in the cold, along with the restless, dissatisfied wind that seemed to change the location of the sycamores. I expected reproaches because I had mentioned the word love, but you only accused me of stealing your pencil, and sadness disappeared with sense. You made a ceremony out of holding your head in your hands because, you said, it could not be contained in itself.

*

If we could just go on walking through these woods and let the pine branches brush our faces, living would still make beads of sweat on your forehead, but you wouldn't have to worry about what you call my exhibitionism. All you liked about trees was the way the light came through the leaves in sheets of precise, parallel rays, like slant rain. This may be an incomplete explanation of our relation, but we've always feared the dark inside the body. You agree there could be no seduction if the structures of propositions did not stand in a physical relation, so that we could get from one to the other. Even so, not every moment of happiness is to hang one's clothes on.

*

I might have known you wouldn't talk to me. But to claim you just didn't want to disguise your thoughts! We've walked along this road before, I said, though perhaps in heavier coats not designed to reveal the form of the body. Later, the moon came out and threw the shadows of branches across the street where they remained, broken. Feverishly you examined the tacit conventions on which conversation depends. I sighed as one does at night, looking down into the river. I wondered if by throwing myself in I could penetrate to the essence of its character, or should I wait for you to stab me as you had practiced in your dream? You said this question, like most philosophical problems, arose from failing to understand the tale of the two youths, two horses, and two lilies. You could prove to me that the deepest rivers are, in fact, no rivers at all.

*

From this observation we turned to consider passion. Looking at the glints of light on the water, you tried to make me tell you not to risk the excitement—to recommend cold baths. The lack of certainty, of direction, of duration, was its own argument, unlike going into a bar to get drunk and getting drunk. Your face was alternately hot and cold, as if translating one language into another—gusts from the storm in your heart, the pink ribbon in your pocket. Its actual color turned out to be unimportant, but its presence disclosed something essential about membranes. You said there was still time, you could still break it off, go abroad, make a movie. I said (politely, I thought) this wouldn't help you. You'd have to kill yourself.

*

Tearing your shirt open, you drew my attention to three dogs in a knot. This served to show how something general can be recorded in unpedigreed notation. I pointed to a bench by a willow, from which we could see the gas tanks across the river, because I thought a bench was a simple possibility: one could sit on it. The black hulks of the tanks began to sharpen in the cold dawn light, though when you leaned against the railing I could smell your hair, which ended in a clean round line on your neck, as was the fashion that year. I had always resented how nimble your neck became whenever you met a woman, regardless of rain falling outside or other calamities. Now, at least, you hunched your shoulders against the shadow of doubt.

*

This time of day, hesitation can mean tottering on the edge, just before the water breaks into the steep rush and spray of the fall. What could I do but turn with the current and get choked by my inner speed? You tried to breathe against the acceleration, waiting for the air to consent. All the while, we behaved as if this search for a pace were useful, like reaching for a plank or wearing rain coats. I was afraid we would die before we could make a statement, but you said that language presupposed meaning, which would be swallowed by the roar of the waterfall.

*

Toward morning, walking along the river, you tossed simple objects into the air which was indifferent around us, though it moved off a little, and again as you put your hand back in your pocket to test the degree of hardness. Everything else remained the same. This is why, you said, there was no fiction.

Conversation 1: On the Horizontal

My mother, she says, always spread, irresistibly, across the entire room, flooding me with familiarity to breed content. I feared my spongy nature and, hoping for other forms of absorption, opened the window onto more water, eyes level with its surface. And lower, till the words "I am here" lost their point with the vanishing air. Just as it's only in use that a proposition grinds its lens.

Deciphering, he says, is not a horizontal motion. Though the way a sentence is meant can be expressed by an expansion that becomes part of it. As a smile may wide-open a door. Holding the tools in my mouth I struggle uphill, my body so perfectly suspended between my father's push and gravity's pull that no progress is made. As if consciousness had to stay embedded in carbon. Or copy. Between camp and bomb. But if you try to sound feelings with words, the stone drops into reaches beyond fathoms.

I *am* here, she says, I've learned that life consists in fitting my body to the earth's slow rotation. So that the way I lean on the parapet betrays dried blood and invisible burns. My shadow lies in the same direction as all the others, and I can't jump over it. My mother's waves ran high. She rode them down on me as on a valley, hoping to flush out the minerals. But I hid my bones under sentences expanding like the flesh in my years.

Language, he says, spells those who love it, sliding sidelong from word to whole cloth. The way fingers extend the body into adventure, print, lakes, and Dead-man's-hand. Wherever the pen pushes, in the teeth of fear and malediction, even to your signature absorbing you into sign. A discomfort with the feel of home before it grows into inflamed tissue and real illness. With symptoms of grammar, punctuation, subtraction of soul. And only death to get you out.

Conversation 2: On the Vertical

We must decipher our lives, he says, forward and backward, down through cracks in the crystal to excrement, entrails, formation of cells. And up. The way the lark at the end of night trills vertically out of the grass—and even that I know too vaguely, so many blades and barely sharper for the passing of blindness—up into anemic heights, the stand-still of time. Could we call this God? or meaning?

The suck of symbol, rather, she quotes. Or an inflection of the voice? Let the song go on. And time. My shadow locks my presence to the ground. It's real enough and outside myself, though regularly consumed at high noon. So maybe I should grant the shoot-out: light may flood me too, completely. But it won't come walking in boots and spurs, or flowing robes, and take my hand or give me the finger with the assurance of a more rational being. And my body slopes toward yours no matter how level the ground.

If we can't call it God, he says, it still perches on the mind, minting strangeness. How could we recognize what we've never seen? A whale in through the window, frame scattered as far as non-standard candles. The sky faints along the giant outline, thar she blows under your skin, tense, a parable right through the body that remains so painfully flesh.

So pleasurably flesh, she says, and dwells among us, flesh offered to flesh, thick as thieves, beginning to see. Even the lark's soar breaks and is content to drop back into yesterday's gravity. Which wins out over dispersion, even doubt, and our thoughts turn dense like matter. The way the sky turns deep honey at noon. The way my sensations seem to belong to a me that has always already sided with the world.

Conversation 3: On Vertigo

That's why thought, he says, means fear. Sicklied o'er with the pale cast. And the feel of a woman. No boundary or edge. No foothold. Blast outspins gravity, breath to temples, gut to throat, propositions break into gasps. Then marriage. The projectile returns to the point of firing. Shaken, I try to take shelter in ratios of dots on a screen.

A narrow bed, she says. Easier to internalize combustion under a hood while rain falls in sheets, glazing a red wheelbarrow for the hell of it. I don't bait fabled beasts to rise to the surface of intonation. But I once watched a rooster mate, and he felt hard inside me, a clenched fist, an alien rock inside me, because there was no thinking to dissolve him. So to slide down, so unutterably, so indifferent.

I don't understand, he says, how manifest destiny blows west with the grass, how the word "soul" floats through the language the way pollen pervades tissue. Worry pivots in the gut, a screeching brake, so scant the difference between mistake and mental disturbance. Is language our cock-adoodledoo? Is thinking a search for curves? Do I need arrowheads or dreadlocks to reach my rawest thoughts? A keyboard at their edge?

The longer I watched, she says, the more distinctly did I feel the snap of that shot flat inside me. So simple the economy of nature: space appears along with matter. So to slide down and stand there. Such self-gravity. So narrow the gap between mistake and morning sickness.

Conversation 4: On Place

I sit in my own shadow, she says, the way my mother gave birth to it. In artificial light, blinds drawn against the darkness of power. I think of you as if you were that shadow, a natural enclosure, a world, not a slight, so I can wander through your darkness. Has our contract inverted time, made our universe contract, a cramped bed for two? And when I say your name, do I draw water, a portrait, curtain, bridge, or conclusion?

Place there is none, he quotes. Not even to hang up our archetypes. Let alone Star Spangled Banners. We go forward and backward, and there is no place. Therefore it is a name for God. My eye, steadfast on traffic lights, abolishes the larger part of the round world. I should look at my feet. Space sweeps through us, a hell of distances bathed in the feeble glow of emptiness. Outward mobility, unimpeded. Suddenly we're nobody home, without any need of inattention, imposture, or talent for deceit.

The wind whips my skin as if it were water, she says. My skin *is* water. For wind read wind, news, sky falling. Is it a mental disturbance or the higher math of love if I hear you talking under my breath and from the torn fragments assume the sun is far away and small, and a look can cause a burn? Superstition, too, is a kind of understanding, and to forego it may have consequences.

Clusters of possibilities whiz through our head, he says. Electric charges, clogged highway, screeching brakes, a house too full of guests. With grounds for disagreement and miscarriage. The light rushes in dry, screaming. But the opaque parts of the nerve oppose the noise and void the options. Then the project must be prolonged in terms of lack.

The Grandeur of the Mountains

Could the grandeur of the mountains be inhaled by a village girl? How fraught the bond between warm-blooded animals. The governing classes had no intention of loosening their grip. The more snow piled up unde-nied on the snowbank the more shadows of clouds moved across "household slavery." What does it mean to put a word between quotation marks? Thanks to the discoveries of Darwin the structural plan of every species is laid down in two strands.

How wonderfully the air is laid down on shadows. She had left her wid-owed mother to discover the grandeur of the mountains. Above a certain solitude no trees grow. Snowballing denoted making few concessions to women. What is passed from generation to generation is a structure of detail like the lacing of boots. Whereas inverted commas take their distance from language.

Such as the accessories of light, heat, electricity, laced boots. Soon she was pregnant. The more rapidly commas were snowballing the harder the resolve to maintain symbols of order. For proper understanding use distance from language. Sometimes slight errors occur above a certain solitude. The sense has been shifted, but not cut into mouthfuls.

This air, then, those we call animals suck in by mouthfuls. In October, there was a severe storm among the symbols of order. This is what is known as genetic mutation. Solitude engulfed the accessories. The vast, shifting grandeur of the mountains. Sexual tolerance was confined within commas, suspended within its history, weighted and therefore thought.

The old woman knew her daughter was near her time. Air is decomposed in the lungs and therefore thought. But genes are grouped into larger units called history. The word enclosed within quotation marks is waiting for its moment of revenge. The governing classes did not confine covert storms, but fidelity to one's wife remained a warm-blooded option. No smoke rising in the public realm.

Part of what they inhale is distributed with the arterial blood (warm). The broken door banged backwards and forwards on its hinges. Only in exceptional cases does a mutation enable an organism to adapt more profitably to solitude. She wrapped her daughter in a quilt. The clergy showed themselves unprepared to overturn the institution of "household slavery." He who puts a word in quotation marks can no longer rid himself of it.

A Form of Lingering

for Lyn Hejinian

To rub together green names and yellow sense-perceptions with thought and feeling. The thing itself transcending language. And nevertheless possible only in language. If not material can it still, in a sentence, be placed next to?

Bronze horses, you write, encounter, possible confusion, thought toward the unthinkable, as spring to cruelty, foxtail, pair of socks, not very wide.

Whether our actions—or was it words—issue from us or come flying like birds to multiply the moment. It isn't now that you could answer.

How to recall the body to itself, with lines discontinuous, metonymy restless, the mirror in back of the head? The sayable may remain unsaid in what is said, but still pulls. The force of gravity or tears.

The sun underlined, you write, not an edge, conjunction, iron filings, feathers, hedgehog, half an egg, cloud, context, launched into, and went west.

Words emitted like knots undone in time. Motes, eyes, neighbors, beams, ownership, weapons of mass destruction.

Not only have we heard all, but still can't prove the length of coastlines by the length of our ruler. Wild horses rush across the plains.

Windmills, you write, Chinese, parachutes, person, nuisance, white curtain on a rod, the full moon falls, black with life, as it continued.

As a subject cut off from everything alien would become blind residue, the line lives through its own estrangement, pause or rose. Relationships of practiced loss then shift within the skin.

A measure of the planetary system. Even if the knowable gets lost in what is known, being a woman means impetus, velocity if not location, or else whistling in your ear.

Learned to type, you write, blankets, pigs, bricklayer, lonely in the foothills, forest fire, discursive from the center, outside pronoun, a moment yellow, and most pleasing discord.

The Body in the Word

for Christopher Middleton

It is not simple. It is opposite. Like revelation or dream. It does not lurk behind its signs. Full of fields, even when alone. Even if you rest all afternoon in a kingdom of caresses it engenders choreographies. And the voice goes deep.

Archipelagos, you write, where begin, armadillos, gloves, a cart with apples, song and pollen, rock wing, labyrinthine nests, a different game.

It is essentially. It could not be other. In the beginning absolutely. Not how the world is, it could not say. But that it exists, the word. Supreme visibility in deepest darkness. As children we kept our secret and grew old. With nudity exhausted.

As for birds, you write, beside me, abyssal glossolalia, soup, brass handles, too early in the day, formation of geese, grammar, not confession, landscape of possibles.

Nothing could be without it. It was made by us. But the nervous system speaks no known language. Roots burst out of the ground and we stumble, jolting the marriage of skeleton and flesh.

Mumblers all, you write, spit and babble, one way sun, inch into the open, mirrors on string, scent bottles, black walls, black kitchen table, in Bamberg, touch everything.

It says nothing. It shows itself. St. Augustine was interested. Words, that is to say, no foundation. Variables crowd the lines of perception, brushing off flies, the time stolen. The body expands. Orgasm not certain.

Pieces that do not fit the puzzle, you quote, sizes, shapes, launch into space, if a round mat, sigh with pleasure, *le nu provençal*, life takes a long look, a birth and its clarity.

Marjorie Welish

By opening the lyric poem to analytical and critical instrumentalites of thought, writing creates a discursive lyric that challenges the stereotype. That the lyric poem issue from a voice, that the voice be an utterance commensurate with feeling, that the voice assume a lyricism for its musical delivery—these characteristics were put to the test in the several compelling modernities that theorized the lyric otherwise.

The song's givens disassembled and furthering other worlds through critical thought have indeed come to represent a changed problematic. "The World Map" is re-presenting the lyric through philosophical reflection; "Weeping Branch" argues for historical skepticism toward lyricism rather than a wholesale identification with the lyrical mode; "[translation] [translation]" proposes that subjectivity need not be first-person singular, need not be spontaneous. Doubled and decidedly mediated, the song has issued from a literary tradition, after all.

The literariness of the lyric poem, then, is a ground, yet also a language for a critical augmentation of poetic possibility. The devices that make a poem literature can themselves be investigated, engaged, and thus refreshed. To formalist investigations add others that explore writing and reading, and the conventional assumptions that have clustered around these practices. Then contemplate that temporal sophistication issuing from music in the modern era has increased the musical offerings for the lyric poem yet also has changed our soundscape. While we are at it, let us note that the concept of expressivity is defined as broadly as possible in the field of aesthetics to mean interpretation: an interpretive rather than a descriptive treatment of a topic. Under these auspices, literariness seems not so restrictive. Especially when enfolded into poetics, which in turn presupposes certain historical or cultural horizons, the lyric poem has much more to do than to hum a few bars of "O Sole Mio."

Lyric and conjectural discourses acknowledge each other in the literary theory of our moment. That is to say, explanation is no longer the secure instrumentality in literary studies it once was; but now, deemed relatively true and subject to changing historical situations and cultural frames, explanation seems reconfigured as interpretation. Theories of interpretation are generative of ways of writing. These days deconstruction sings of its speculative skepticism, even as cultural studies written in aphoristic fragments has entered its second century. Poetics itself has become a subject for exploring the potentiality of literature, with its signifying system open to question.

Respected, Feared, and Somehow Loved

In the long run we must fix our compass,
and implore our compass,
and arraign our shadow play in heaven, among the pantheon
where all the plea-bargaining takes place.
Within the proscenium arch,
the gods negotiate ceaselessly,
and the words he chooses to express the baleful phrase dare to be
    obsessed
with their instrumentality. Please send for our complete catalogue.

As in the days of creation, the clouds gossip and argue, the gods waver.
The gods oversee such unstable criteria as fourthly, fifthly.
The rest are little timbral touches.
The gods waver. To reiterate a point, the gods oversee
the symposium on the life raft—a crazed father, a dead son;
an unwarranted curtailment of family.

Part of the foot, and thus part of the grace splinter in dismay,
and the small elite of vitrines where our body parts are stored
dies in a place crash in Mongolia.
Why didn't someone do something to stop the sins of the climate,
and earlier,

why did not someone rewrite the sins of the vitrines, the windows
shipwrecked icily, the windows called away?

Veil

An enchanted frame assures the image of a loved one.
Then there is the question of response.
A loved one produces things. Then there is this question
of existence.
                    Motion dashed to the ground,
and now a hapless pattern in its stead.
Little portions of liveliness are thrown out as inquiries.

Then there is the day that lives up to its preconceived ideas.
Then there is the day
empowered to train all sense on the moment,
holding onto that bias, often and later;
                                        although meanwhile,
the day is in position and empowered the senses
to caress the starstruck flames,
the excited jets surrounding these inquiries.

                                If there is a pattern
of stars beyond the starstruck blue, it spells desire,
and beyond this, a paler tendency
for stars to sift a desire to be anywhere, and you
not even among them in question form.

Skin

Our skin: strenuously tutored to appreciate the vernacular
body a feeling might have. Companies
of hands, legs, cigarettes, a whip, the sea
tangle in the mutilated lamplight,

and wrap an intelligent enterprise in a gang of approaches.
I think that black into pink is devastating. A bitter winter,
the whip, the sea—all familiar rubble that comes around nightly,
but so familiar, the feeling need only mention surrender and we
    surrender.

In the postwar victory, lamplight is harsher, categorical.
Pink is devastating, a stone lawn.
A great part of the American pavilion
has been given to an iron blue and magnificent écorché—

the spirit, when the spirit is flayed and forbidden
to talk about itself. It feels normal
to live in the present amid musculature
of beautiful early work propped against an uphill sea.

Moses und Aron

Entirety.
Inquiry.

Sunken revelation
minus the idolatry

and bacchanalian click-track:
where is ought?

Schönberg asks of this mien,
of this cabinet

impaired to shed light.

Entirety somehow annulled
qualitatively through inquiet,

optimum warmth. Anathema
corresponding to gold

mimesis,
mind. Where is rival

dumbfoundedness?

The entirety hammering outside
the fool.

An appeal to
sounding that note.

You were omniscient a moment ago.
To beguile many and be beguiled by one

incompatibility.
Why?

Schönberg asks.
Screams, laughter, silences.

Do you wish to escape without saving this page?

Dumbfoundedness?
discolored now in laughter.

Screams, laughter where there is enigma
or the onset of the nearby, discolored now,

disinterred many times as they parody ultramarine,
the sun, the sun's disappearance.

Move What? To Where?
Unimaginable, omnipresent, eternal,

stay far from us.
Move What? *Staff, law; serpent, wisdom.* To Where?

Now this God can be imagined.

The World Map

Prospect in readiness, together with
the annexation of processes,
     revealing-dissembles

landslides or pure lyric
by which to complete the fragmented prayer "as intended."

Dumping gravel
    on emancipated frontiers. . . .

If H.B. really were
darkening a bildungsroman of irony, he would say of R.R.
he is second,
    that he is the second most interesting philosopher,

or that the tenderness of located
skimming stones
    across pain and dust

"helps us get what we antecedently decided."

A landslide
    idling in the mirror . . .

[translation]

In the song embargo

one falls back analogously, analogously fond
of glad method
to investigate 'I' and its matrix.

A song decomposing

through aria cultivated in any amount, and much with gloved voice-over into which the authentic "I" has been admitted briefly as an apprehension. Unseen in many films, she is.

A song

peculiar to the discursive level.

[translation]

In an elongated opera of pleats, grafts in skeptical
voice, voice is

"I" sing of the song embargo.
Ploughed under aria and set against recitative are vocal
grafts—of epic, novella, now
of a rubbing in sound requiring broad definition
within which goes the bass-baritone Hakan Hagegard, even

as thin voices vaporized
vaporized the crescent of a child's light voice.

Elizabeth Willis

A poetics

I would place my work among those who recognize an evolving relation to both the "traditional" and the "new" and who tend to recognize *as* new this reconfiguring of or re-engagement with traditions. (I mean traditions broadly to include anything from Thucydides to John Greenleaf Whittier to Oulipo.) For me, poetry at its best produces enormous polymorphous joy. I love textual labor, the apparent limitlessness of textual depth. I'm interested less in the fact that there are endless ways of producing text than in the potentiality *within* a text, the way that even a small poem can spin out an entire industry of meanings, music, and cultural critique.

Maybe what I find so interesting within the work of my peers stems from the fact that we emerged as writers in a time when the canon was being actively destabilized in various ways. Given that instability, we had to read widely and develop our own critical opinions about poetry on both ends of the tradition & innovation continuum. In the work of my close contemporaries I also see—and identify with—a vital drive to preserve or remake culture. An urgent naming of the things that compose the present moment, grasped in an instant before they go out of print or are forgotten and replaced by additional "information." To my mind part of what's so interesting about the current moment is its refusal of an overtly oedipal relation to literary traditions on either the right or the left, and a willingness to construct and invent not only new kinds of poetry but new ways of reading.

The Tree of Personal Effort

after Charles Rennie Mackintosh

The lost highway of ornament fades into origin. Shipwrecks return like magnets to their builders. In the tree of personal effort, a balloon is lodged or branches are basketed. What did we think we dared to sail away from, an unread book, an aspirin? My body knew I was anchored to earth with flesh. Build a bigger bellows if you want to rise above your life. So sighs the pilot's cloud of word. To imply or intone the whole possibility of human sun. The rose rose unknit with spring. A dragonfly in your hand for luck.

Arthur in Egypt

Where do you go after a season in Denver? Walking through Africa in shoes of sand. My name was a green flash on the glassy horizon. My pen leaked until there was nothing else to say. When my feet were gone I rowed ashore, beached on the word, *pure.* What happens once can never come again, even in a dream. So I moved on, or it passed through.

Three Apples, Two Chestnuts, Bowl, and Silver Goblet; or, The Silver Goblet

after Chardin; for Lisa Jarnot

As in the darkly open science of the foreground, sheepishly at rest as upon air; the rest we stand in. We stand in for the chestnuts, a type of their magnetism, reflecting on the room; or upon the average darkness, aristocratic brown, with hunted things; we come to rest among them. The painted room, locked in a type of kindness. We reflect upon this lovely habit of this hare with whom we are, in the habit of this picture, getting caught. To hide the virtues of a boundless leaping, we regard reflection in the chestnut. As if the painter drew himself as Death into the still life; as of a sculptural stillness, commas in the dark. A figure of ourselves reflected or a type of picture resting; sheepishly as air, locked in a form of capture.

Constable's Day Off

Loving the human bird—
the bright converse
of yellow-flowered grasses—
why aren't we lying
in miles of weedy clover?
The bright boat, tumbling through it
the blue of it—Or,
taking the kid out of the picture
(what you loved to see)
a girl who talks to birds—Don't go
Let's delay or—like Shakespeare—"fly"
all disappointment
in the green and untidy
molecular air

Drive

Trouble fell weeping at the sight of paved-over love. Distinctions that hold branches apart against sky, seeing it through lenses, or even the eye if round. The final heat of a negative drifting off the road, inside outside. I fell I snowed I conjured into not. Fixed annoyance, detailed love. Sinkers, undesperate, are always the last donut. And this once pair, a final spelling in figments of polish, of door.

*

Felt things last longer than seen things. Says who, drawing out forks of fire, who walking by, tied for departure, packaged into powder. Fled ecstasy as a response like "brilliant" can mean anything. Everything appears to shine given enough darkness. Crushed into brilliance, the bright ball, dished. Write your poem in the space above, erasing what is beneath it. Paper covers rock. Listen. It's tough, hearts get crushed by metal these days, no matter what.

*

What last broke against leaf, under leaf-bearing mind? So little disturbs the sea by comparison. Do you mind? Finding a reflected mountain is really a shadow, a tree is beneath its color, the shore a mirage. A real boat in imaginary water. Yellow fall, green gilled. Trees have the only real land-legs. Consider our end. The lights are dry in daylight, up in the dipper, the Hammer, scorpion, the Hurricane. The kid's fire is hidden, underneath. To crawl out from under. It's dirt. Don't win. Don't put it out.

*

Haze horns in with ire for summer. Even bad dreams spill through into morning: waxy cylinders of belted sunlight. We Never Close. A western anthem. In my mother's mouth are many scansions, but earthliness has something wanting in spite of its honey. When I was a bud I hustled sandbags for a quarter. I wore the bell. I sent or sat among daisies. Translate the dollar. Follow that pen. Fall for piffle, yet. I miss the town that born me.

*

Girl goes home, goes down, a slippery symptom. Boy declines behind haircut, unfair across its table, vast, flat, table, tipping, lost, left, a peach. Free in time and heart before four, they're mediterranean, a listed number. Particular, open, improbable, lichen, long eared, overhead, parallel. I hear the clanging just out of reach, my thought following. Bitten by. Broke. It's too young, the rose that blocks my window. I mean to last.

*

What you rise out of may not be dirt, but what you breathe must be air. On an indigo chart, we drive without a future, left to wish outside the forward rush of things. Who would not leave the mess for the illumination, the culture for the poem? Believe in inconstancy, a colorist. Forgetting the orangist is only a pomologist, not a painter sent home for lack of design. The night's a plateau. Where would we be in desert night, deserted. Constantinopolized. Oranged.

*

Valley genes screening for dust, pump off beauty for a bite. A patinaed stream gutting noon. A town coined with lace. Is it a dove in mourning or homo erectus on a roll to the Genghis Kitchen? Blowing oreward, open-handed, in faulted nature, flushed. An excellent copy, reluctantly boarded. Slightly foxed. Otherwise, fine.

*

A curtained battle prize of me, not-me, shaken into sweat. A drive-in ecstasy of float, throated. Is disingenuity a glimpse of fabrication, or the lie of nature, satinized, distinct, in linen life? A livid feature of face arranged on plastic, shadowed or ennumbered. An alpine trigger draped in product. The girl missed or missing. The surface of painted water is riddled with oars, a bridge crowned with bullets for thorns.

*

A fool by nature, daylight beats me up. A trim surrender coughing out lemons. A tear of summer gasoline or an insect chipping away at morning, caught in my ear. Maybe it's not the tool I wanted. Digging my mother for her fortitude, my father for lasting. Everything has a pattern, but that's not all in the little white room, asleep in the drift, the life on paper.

*

In simple shade an indigent itinerary is lost against the effort
to get there. A feel copped then forgotten. An echo afforded
from, I couldn't guess. Built, fanatical landscape; unheralded
heroic absences. Figured out plainly in numbers or sticking
the mind with words. Ticking out like native stuffing,
wishing in a wing, exiting right or left; sticking around. I
give up the song. It hides. It wants the plum I never had, in
a metaphorical garden, forgetting its naked self, no longer
nude.

*

The day left off with a kind of singing "bang." Goldenrod
in a small sea-like air, specific and unbroken. I cannot favor
hunger or its alternatives. I cannot describe salt. In a parallel
universe does anything intersect the confused blossoming
blueness of a wall that is not sea, not goldenrod, but the
paper fastening of you, standing against it? I favor concrete
between our rage and its mirage. Its broken line. Catch the
flying saucer but spit out its metal mystery. Adore the big
green nothing of the past, the rationing of calm late in the
century, like the arches of a brick heart, letting go.

On the Resemblance of Some Flowers to Insects

A smoky vessel drifts east like a slippery elixir. By simple
rotation night collapses with its head in the dirt, though
from the heights it appears more like cubist swagger.
Suddenly curtains. What lives in a room takes on the
spirit of the room. This is true even of television. Imagine
deciding the gully a life will follow as if choosing breakfast
over diligent labor. I don't remember my first brush with
pollen, yet I've watched words flower sideways across your
mouth. In a month we'll be dizzily older. Moths will leave
singed paper on the stoop. Is this my design? An ant crosses
my shadow so many times looking for its crumb, I think

it's me who's needlessly swaying. Its path is busy eloquence while I'm merely armed, like a chair leaving the scent of large things on the breeze.

The Great Egg of Night

Infancy moons us with its misty cloudcover, an updraft nearly laundered of intent. Palmed and tendered in subaltern shade, I could not shake the memory of a train that whitely striped the hills. The surrendering pike pours out in uniform. Butter-gloved epiphanies slide past us in their muscle car. In the words of the daffodil, am I in my kerchief more lovely than this ash kicking up against the wheel? What form do women take? Or is she taken like a path to frosty metaphor, a seed easier crushed than opened? Can a word be overturned by jest, or does it take a wayward spark to fire up your arsenal of lace? The darkest blue is black, felt around the edges. I give the cool a running start, a catching chance, rigging our descent to decent landings, piloting home.

The Steam Engine

I came back to the meadow an unsuspecting hart, trying to wake up from a long night of walking. I was looking for a subtext, a heavy horsy bee doing battle with its inclination. What's your angle? A little evanescent on the rim, it's only a willow, beaked and shining, a toothy margin holding up banks. Have we overstayed our party in the heavenly city or are we spilling through its gates trying not to get trampled? On the berm I filled a basket with crashing birds. In the dream you pointed sideways with your thumb where the cars were flying.

A Description of the Poison Tree

The girl is a grid, silked with phenomena, an early promise broken into clover. An owl bends both its eyes to this object. Her desire for shining, a symptom of this bashfulness. Among the lower orders a W is sibilant. A physical lantern, honey in the ear. A larger bird's cry may be hidden from view by a broad enough table. I find her in delirium about to pass for mad. The letter S between the teeth, pushed back into the mouth, as when confronted she has pointed to the word "paper." She doesn't want to be the dollar sign, split and smirking, living in a desert of bolted-down things.

Her Mossy Couch

I stain lengthwise all I touch. The world is so touching, seen this way, in fleshtones, aggrieved, gleaming as the lights go out, looking in to the crease of relativity. We've seen this before, why? Triumph arches over us like bad emotion. We were supposed to feel more connected to it, we were supposed to feel humanly moved by imaginary strings. All the words in the world are moving pictures to the dizzy ear, fleas, inadequate deceptions of nocturnal air, pushing buttons, pushing papers, pushing pedals up the long hill. Who could get over the blatant radiance of a name like Doris Day, throwing your finest features into political relief, a warehouse in the shadow of apples and streams.

Ferns, Mosses, Flags

We all live under the rule of Pepsi, by the sanctified waters of an in-ground pond. Moss if it gathers is a sign of shifting weathers, the springing scent of consensual facts. A needle's knowing drops into focus while you sleep in its haystack. A boy on the road, a guileless girl disguised as a brook. Even trees deploy their shadows, embossing your skin with the sound of freedom breaking. No one mistakes choice for necessity. Look at the pilgrims in your filmy basket, illustrious eyebrows colored with chalk. The lake is panicking. A latent mystery detected in sepia is quaking to its end. I too have a family, astonished, unsaintly. Asleep, I saw them. A porcelain dome insisting on trust, jeweled with telepathy. I don't know how to pour this country from a thinner vessel. Or account for the era of Martian diplomacy, its cheap labor. Little bridges connect every century, seasonally covered with the rime of empire. Can you successfully ignore the eyes in the painting? Can you recount the last three images in reverse order? I read the picture and did what it told me, ducking through the brush with my tablet and pen, following some star.

Why No New Planets are Ejected from the Sun

These our ships are the copies of copies. This x is that, lifting off the dock. We think we're here because we're crouching in the umber of syllables, that sun is "killing me," a flag among flies, our frozen boat in frozen oil. Let's haunt the beach instead of this history beset with cosmic jelly. At the blind is it morning already? The word has meant so many things, I need a fence to move this gem-like feeling. Or I'm that bus, in hacked-up disquiet, stuck at the light.

19 Short Films about John Wesley Hardin

I draw the scene in red and black with both hands. I, John Wesley, speaking with his gun, pivoting left to draw right. John Wesley saw the wheel. It was inside him sawing away. Fire is a sixth sense reaching out to protect our back. The yellow blast of this instinctual arm. Between Moscow and London I killed a man and scared a woman. A hard case moving westly. I'm alive and against it, genuine reflex, gemini redux, a dark eraser in blonde culture. I loved Sal, but Sal loved mutton. My greatest pleasure, a lone-headed jane. Before I leave my early days, I was scared by nothing but a ghost or lightening. I nearly killed the boy who said I wrote a bad poem. God's pluck against the drink, here I was pinched by a plague of ticks. Mage still showed fight in the person of a spitting bet, but Bill would have myself in the night. Near Pisgah, I loved the word, I taught in the Old Word schoolhouse, I never stammered. I am still, in a tight, moving somewhere fast. This horse is not mine.

Contributor Notes

Bruce Beasley is the author of six collections of poems, including *Lord Brain* (winner of the University of Georgia Press Contemporary Poetry Series competition), *Summer Mystagogia* (selected by Charles Wright for the 1996 Colorado Prize), and most recently *The Corpse Flower: New and Selected Poems*. He has won fellowships from the National Endowment for the Arts and the Artist Trust, and three Pushcart prizes. He is a professor of English at Western Washington University.

Martine Bellen's most recent poetry collection is *GHOSTS!* (Spuyten Duyvil Press). Other collections include *Further Adventures of the Monkey God* (Spuyten Duyvil Press); *The Vulnerability of Order* (Copper Canyon Press); *Tales of Murasaki and Other Poems* (Sun & Moon Press), which won the National Poetry Series Award; and *Places People Dare Not Enter* (Potes & Poets Press).

Mei-mei Berssenbrugge was born in Beijing and grew up in Massachusetts. She is the author of twelve books of poetry. Her selected poems, *I Love Artists*, was published by the University of California Press in 2006. She lives in rural New Mexico and in New York City.

Gillian Conoley's latest collection, *Profane Halo*, was published by Wave Books. Her previous collections include *Lovers in the Used World*; *Tall Stranger*, a finalist for the National Book Critics' Circle Award; *Beckon*; and *Some Gangster Pain*, winner of the Great Lakes Colleges New Writer Award. She is a recipient of the Jerome J. Shestack Poetry Prize from *The American Poetry Review*, as well as several Pushcart Prizes. Her work has been anthologized widely, most recently in Norton's new *American Hybrid*, *Best American Poetry* and *The Body Electric, America's Best Poetry from The American Poetry Review*. Her work has been translated into Italian, Spanish, and French. Professor and Poet-in-Residence at Sonoma State University, she is the founder and editor of *Volt*. She lives in the San Francisco Bay Area.

Kathleen Fraser's most recent books include *W I T N E S S* (2007, Chax Press); *Discrete Categories Forced into Coupling* (2004, Apogee Press); and *hi dde violeth i dde violet* (2004, Nomados Press). Her collected essays, *Translating the Unspeakable, Poetry and the Innovative Necessity*, were published in 2000 by the University of Alabama Press. *il cuore: the heart, Selected Poems, 1970–1995*, was published in 1997 by Wesleyan University Press. Fraser has also collaborated on three artist's books with painters. From 1983 to 1992 she published and edited *HOW(ever)*, a journal devoted to innovative women's writing. Fraser is winner of a Guggenheim and two NEA Fellowships in Poetry, and the Frank O'Hara Award for innovative achievement. She currently teaches in the graduate writing program at the California College of the Arts and lives for five months of each year in Rome.

Forrest Gander is a writer and translator whose most recent books include *Eye Against Eye* (poems, New Directions 2005), *A Faithful Existence: Reading, Memory, and Transcendence* (essays, Shoemaker and Hoard 2005), *Firefly Under the Tongue: Selected Poems of Coral Bracho* (translation, New Directions 2008), and *As a Friend* (novel, New Directions 2008). He is a Professor of English and Comparative Literature at Brown University.

C. S. Giscombe was born in 1950 in Dayton, Ohio and attended the State University of New York at Albany and Cornell University. His full length poetry books are *Postcards* (1977), *Here* (1994), and *Giscome Road* (1998); his book of linked essays, *Into and Out of Dislocation*, was published in 2000. His poetry has been anthologized in the *Best American Poetry* and Pushcart Prize anthologies, in *The Oxford Anthology of African-American Poetry*, and elsewhere. Books in progress include a prose work about public transportation, *Railroad Sense*, and a poetry book, *Prairie Style*, about the American Midwest. Mr. Giscombe is a long-distance cyclist and expects to complete training for his railroad engineer's license in 2008. He lives in the Bay Area and teaches English at the University of California at Berkeley.

Peter Gizzi's books include *The Outernationale, Some Values of Landscape and Weather, Artificial Heart,* and *Periplum and other poems 1987–92.* He has also published several limited-edition chapbooks, folios, and artist books. His honors include the Lavan Younger Poet Award from the Academy of American Poets (1994) and fellowships in poetry from the Howard Foundation (1998), the Foundation for Contemporary Arts (1999), and the Guggenheim Foundation (2005). His editing projects have included *o*bl_k: a journal of language arts, Exact Change Yearbook,* and *The House That Jack Built: The Collected Lectures of Jack Spicer.* He teaches at the University of Massachusetts at Amherst.

Brenda Hillman has published seven collections of poetry, all from Wesleyan University Press, the most recent of which are *Loose Sugar* (1997), *Cascadia* (2001), and *Pieces of Air in the Epic* (2005), which won the 2005 William Carlos Williams Prize for Poetry. She has edited an edition of Emily Dickinson's poetry for Shambhala Publications, and, with Patricia Dienstfrey, coedited *The Grand Permisson: New Writings on Poetics and Motherhood* (2003). Hillman is the Olivia C. Filippi Professor of Poetry at Saint Mary's College in Moraga, California. She is also involved in non-violent activism as a member of the Code Pink Women for Peace in the San Francisco Bay Area.

Claudia Keelan is the author of four books of poetry, most recently *The Devotion Field* from Alice James Books. She directs the MFA International at the University of Nevada at Las Vegas, where she is also the editor of *Interim* (www.interimmag.org).

Timothy Liu is the author of six books of poems, most recently *For Dust Thou Art.* A new book, *Polytheogamy,* is forthcoming. His journals and papers are archived in the Berg Collection at the New York Public Library. An Associate Professor at William Paterson University and a member of the Core Faculty in Bennington College's Graduate Writing Seminars, Liu lives in Manhattan.

Nathaniel Mackey was born in Miami, Florida, in 1947, and grew up, from age four, in California. He is the author of four books of poetry, most recently *Splay Anthem* (New Directions, 2006), winner of the National Book Award; an ongoing prose work, *From a Broken Bottle Traces of Perfume Still Emanate,* of which four volumes have been published, most recently *Bass Cathedral* (New Directions, 2007); and two books of criticism, most recently *Paracritical Hinge: Essays, Talks, Notes, Interviews* (University of Wisconsin Press, 2005). He edits the literary magazine *Hambone* and coedited, with Art Lange, the anthology *Moment's Notice: Jazz in Poetry and Prose* (Coffee House Press, 1993). He teaches at the University of California, Santa Cruz.

Suzanne Paola's most recent book of poetry, *The Lives of the Saints* , was published by the University of Washington Press in 2002; it was a finalist for the 2003 Lenore Marshall Poetry Prize. Paola's second book, *Bardo,* was published by the University of Wisconsin Press as winner of the press's Brittingham Prize, chosen by Donald Hall, currently the U.S. Poet Laureate. She is also the author of two books of nonfiction and coauthor of a textbook on nonfiction writing, *Tell It Slant: Writing and Shaping Creative Nonfiction.*

Bin Ramke's ninth book, *Tendril,* is from Omnidawn. He edits the *Denver Quarterly* and teaches at the University of Denver and the School of the Art Institute of Chicago.

Donald Revell is Professor of English at the University of Utah in Salt Lake City. From 1988–1994, he was editor-in-chief of *Denver Quarterly* and is now poetry editor of *Colorado Review.* Twice awarded fellowships from the National Endowment for the Arts, he is also a former fellow of the Ingram Merrill and Guggenheim Foundations. Among his many other honors are the Utah Book Award, two Awards in Poetry from the PEN Center USA, and the Lenore Marshall Prize. *Pennyweight Windows: New & Selected Poems* was published in 2005 by Alice James Books, which also published *A Thief of Strings* (2007). Omnidawn published his *Invisible Green: Selected Prose* (2005) as well as his translation of Arthur Rimbaud's *A Season in Hell* (2007). Revell lives in the desert south of Las Vegas with his wife, poet Claudia Keelan, and their children, Benjamin Brecht and Lucie Lou.

Martha Ronk is the author of seven books of poetry, including *In a landscape of having to repeat* (Omnidawn), winner of the 2005 PEN USA award for best poetry book, and *Why/Why Not* (University of California Press, 2003). Her book *Vertigo* was chosen by C. D. Wright for the National Poetry Series and will be published by Coffee House Press. Her residencies include MacDowell and Djerassi, and in 2007 she received an NEA award. She was editor for ten years at Littoral Books and is now co-editor for poetry of *The New Review of Literature*. She is Irma and Jay Price Professor of English at Occidental College in Los Angeles and has also taught in graduate writing programs at the University of Colorado at Boulder, Otis College of Art & Design, and Naropa Institute.

Aaron Shurin is the author of fifteen books, including the poetry collections *Involuntary Lyrics* (Omnidawn, 2005), *The Paradise of Forms: Selected Poems* (Talisman House, 1999), and the prose collections *Unbound: A Book of AIDS* (Sun & Moon, 1997) and *King of Shadows* (forthcoming in 2008 from City Lights). His work has appeared in over twenty national and international anthologies, most recently *Nuova Poesia Americana: San Francisco* (Italy: Oscar Mondadori, 2006) and *Locul nimanui. Antologie de Poezie Americana Contemporana* (Romania: Editura Cartea Romaneasca, 2006). He codirects the MFA in Writing Program at the University of San Francisco.

Carol Snow lives and works in San Francisco, where she was born in 1949. She is the author of *Artist and Model* (National Poetry Series selection, Atlantic Monthly Press), *For*, and *The Seventy Prepositions* (both University of California Press). Work in her new collection, *Placed Karesansui*, draws its form from the dry-landscape garden at Ryoan-ji.

Susan Stewart is the author of five books of poems, most recently *Columbarium*, which won the National Book Critics Circle Award for 2003, and the forthcoming *Red Rover*, both from the University of Chicago Press. She is a former MacArthur Fellow and a current Chancellor of the Academy of American Poets. Her many books of prose include *Poetry and the Fate of the Senses*, which won both the Christian Gauss and Truman Capote prizes for literary criticism, and *The Open Studio: Essays on Art and Aesthetics*. She teaches poetry and aesthetics at Princeton University, where she is Annan Professor of English.

Cole Swensen has published eleven books of poetry, most recently *The Glass Age* (Alice James, 2007). Her 2004 book *Goest* was a finalist for the National Book Award, and other volumes have won the Iowa Poetry Prize, the San Francisco State Poetry Center Book Award, the New American Writing Award, and a National Poetry Series. She's also a translator of contemporary French poetry, prose, and art criticism, and her translation of Jean Fremon's *The Island of the Dead* won the 2004 PEN USA Award for Literary Translation. She's the founder and editor of a new small press, La Presse, and she teaches at the Iowa Writers' Workshop.

Rosmarie Waldrop's trilogy (*The Reproduction of Profiles, Lawn of Excluded Middle,* and *Reluctant Gravities*) has been reprinted by New Directions under the title *Curves to the Apple.* Other recent books of poetry are *Splitting Images* (Zasterle), *Blindsight* (New Directions), and *Love, Like Pronouns* (Omnidawn). Her collected essays, *Dissonance (if you are interested),* was published by University of Alabama Press in 2005. She lives in Providence, Rhode Island, where she coedits Burning Deck books with Keith Waldrop.

Marjorie Welish is the author of *The Annotated "Here" and Selected Poems* and *Word Group* (both from Coffee House Press). *Of the Diagram: The Work of Marjorie Welish* (Slought Books, 2003) gathers essays about her practice in poetry, art, and criticism. As Judith E. Wilson Visiting Poetry Fellow of Cambridge University in 2005, she completed a manuscript *Isle of the Signatories,* which is forthcoming from Coffee House Press in Spring 2008. A Fulbright Senior Specialist, she taught in the American Studies Program at the University of Frankfurt in 2007.

Elizabeth Willis is the author of four books of poetry, *Meteoric Flowers* (Wesleyan, 2006), *Turneresque* (Burning Deck, 2003), *The Human Abstract,* a National Poetry Series winner (Penguin, 1995), and *Second Law* (Avenue B, 1993). She teaches at Wesleyan University.

Acknowledgments

Except where noted, all artist statements are original to this volume, and copyright 2008 by their respective authors.

Bruce Beasley: "The Vanishing Point," from *The Corpse Flower: New and Selected Poems*. Copyright 2006 by Bruce Beasley. Reprinted by permission of the University of Washington Press. "The Scarecrow's Supplication," from *Lord Brain*. Copyright 2005 by Bruce Beasley. Reprinted by permission of the University of Georgia Press.

Martine Bellen: "Terrifying Creatures," "Dream of the Spider Bridge," "Tale of the Ancient Princess," and "Fireflies and Summer Rain," from *Tales of Murasaki and Other Poems*. Copyright 1999 by Martine Bellen. Reprinted by permission of Green Integer.

Mei-mei Berssenbrugge: "Rabbit, Hair, Leaf," from *Random Possession*. Copyright 1979 by Mei-mei Berssenbrugge. Reprinted by permission of the author. "Fog," "Tan Tien," "Safety," "Safety," and "Safety," from *I Love Artists: New and Selected Poems*. Copyright 2006 by Mei-mei Berssenbrugge. Reprinted by permission of the University of California Press.

Gillian Conoley: "The Birth of Beauty" and "We Don't Have to Share a Fate," from *Beckon*. Copyright 1996 by Gillian Conoley. Published by Carnegie Mellon University Press. Reprinted by permission of the author. "Flute Girl," "Alcibiades," and "Socrates," from *Lovers in the Used World*. Copyright 2001 by Gillian Conoley. Reprinted by permission of Carnegie Mellon University Press. "Inelegant Motherless Child" and "Native," from *Profane Halo*. Copyright 2005 by Gillian Conoley. Reprinted by permission of Wave Books.

Kathleen Fraser: "Medusa's hair was snakes. Was thought, split inward," "Notes re: Echo," "Claim," "Losing people," and "Those labdanum hours," from *Il cuore: the heart: Selected Poems 1970–1995*. Copyright 1997 by Kathleen Fraser. Reprinted by permission of Wesleyan University Press. "You can hear her breathing in the photograph," from *Discrete Categories Forced Into Coupling*. Copyright 2004 by Kathleen Fraser. Published by Apogee Press. Reprinted by permission of the author.

Forrest Gander: "Face," "Field Guide to Southern Virginia," "Anniversary," and "Garment of Light," from *Science & Steepleflower*. Copyright 1997 by Forrest Gander. Reprinted by permission of New Directions Publishing Corporation. "To C" and "To Eurydice," from *Torn Awake*. Copyright 2001 by Forrest Gander. Reprinted by permission of New Directions Publishing Corporation. "Ligature 5" and "Ligature 6" copyright 2007 by Forrest Gander. Reprinted by permission of the author.

C. S. Giscombe: "(all time)" and "(Blue Hole)," from *Here*. Copyright 1994 by C. S. Giscombe. Reprinted by permission of Dalkey Archive Press. "(Hand-eye coordination)" and "(The canal)," from *Two Sections from Practical Geography*. Copyright 1999 by C. S. Giscombe. Published by Diaeresis Chapbook Series. Reprinted by permission of the author. "Far," "Favorite Haunt," "Prairie Style," and "Nature Boy," from *Inland*. Copyright 2000 by C. S. Giscombe. Published by Leroy Chapbooks. Reprinted by permission of the author.

Peter Gizzi: "Periplum" and "Nocturne," from *Periplum and other poems*. Copyright 1992, 2004 by Peter Gizzi. Reprinted by permission of Salt Publishing. "Speck," "Lonely Tylenol," and "The Truth & Life of Pronouns," from *Artificial Heart*. Copyright 1998 by Peter Gizzi. Reprinted by permission of Burning Deck. "A History of the Lyric" and "In Denfense of Nothing," from *Some Values of Landscape and Weather*. Copyright 2003 by Peter Gizzi. Reprinted by permission of Wesleyan University Press. "Bolshevescent" and "A Western Garden," from *The Outernationale*. Copyright 2007 by Peter Gizzi. Reprinted by permission of Wesleyan University Press.

Brenda Hillman: "Thicket Group," from *Loose Sugar*. Copyright 1997 by Brenda Hillman. Reprinted by permission of Wesleyan University Press. "Air for Mercury," from *Cascadia*. Copyright 2001 by Brenda Hillman. Reprinted by permission of Wesleyan University Press. "Air in the Epic," from *Pieces of Air in the Epic*. Copyright 2005 by Brenda Hillman. Reprinted by permission of Wesleyan University Press. "Enchanted Twig" (first pubished in *Sonora Review*) and "Partita for Sparrows" (first published in *Modern Review*) copyright 2007 by Brenda Hillman. Reprinted by permission of the author.

Claudia Keelan: "Refinery" and "If Not in the Field Then Where," from *Refinery*. Copyright 1994 by Claudia Keelan. Reprinted by permission of Cleveland State University Poetry Center. "The Modern Life of the Soul," "And Its Discontents," and "While the Wind Speaks," from *The Secularist*. Copyright 1997 by Claudia Keelan. Reprinted by permission of the University of Georgia Press. "Sun Going Down," from *The Devotion Field*. Copyright 2004 by Claudia Keelan. Reprinted by permission of Alice James Books.

Timothy Liu: "In Flagrante Delicto," from *Hard Evidence*. Copyright 2001 by Timothy Liu. Published by Talisman House. Reprinted by permission of the author. "Dau Al Set," "Besieged by Roses Shot from Quivers," "Orpheus at the Threshold," "Overcast," and "Petty," from *For Dust Thou Art*. Copyright 2005 by Timothy Liu. Reprinted by permission of Southern Illinois University Press.

Nathaniel Mackey: "[Waters . . .]", from *Eroding Witness*. Copyright 1986 by Nathaniel Mackey. Published by University of Illinois Press. Reprinted by permission of the author. "Song of the Andoumboulou: 55," "Song of the Andoumboulou: 60," "Sound and Semblance," and "Dread Lakes Aperture," from *Splay Anthem*. Copyright 2006 by Nathaniel Mackey. Reprinted by permission of New Directions Publishing Corporation.

Suzanne Paola: "Calenture and Loom," "The White," and "Daphne," from *Glass*. Copyright 1995 by *Quarterly Review of Literature*. Reprinted by permission of the author. "Red Girl," from *Bardo*. Copyright 1998 by the Board of Regents of the University of Wisconsin System. Reprinted by permission of University of Wisconsin Press. "The Third Letter of St. Paul at the Playground," from *The Lives of the Saints*. Copyright 2002 by

Suzanne Paola. Reprinted by permission of the University of Washington Press. "Eros in Love" copyright 2007 by Suzanne Paola. Reprinted by permission of the author.

Bin Ramke: "No Thing," "The Gods That Sleep in Museums," and "Virtual Sculpture," from *Airs, Waters, Places.* Copyright 2001 by Bin Ramke. Reprinted by permission of the University of Iowa Press. "The Tender Grasses of the Field," "Where the Famous Wish They Had Lived," "Narcissus Old, Anyone Young," "Pain Is the History of Consciousness," "After Virgil," and "Chemical Virtue," from *Matter.* Copyright 2004 by Bin Ramke. Reprinted by permission of the University of Iowa Press. "Been There Done That (Desert Warfare)" and "For the Relations of Words Are in Pairs First," copyright 2007 by Bin Ramke. Reprinted by permission of the author.

Donald Revell: "Dear Friend," from *Invisible Green: Selected Prose.* Copyright 2005 by Donald Revell. Reprinted by permission of Omnidawn Publishing. "Motel View," from *From the Abandoned Cities.* Copyright 1983 by Donald Revell. Reprinted by permission of the author. "Raft of the Medusa," from *The Gaza of Winter.* Copyright 1988 by Donald Revell. Reprinted by permission of the University of Georgia Press. "Apocrypha," "Survey," and "Wartime," from *New Dark Ages.* Copyright 1990 by Donald Revell. Reprinted by permission of Wesleyan University Press. "Anniversary of Many Cities" and "The Massacre of the Innocents," from *Erasures.* Copyright 1992 by Donald Revell. Reprinted by permission of Wesleyan University Press. "Inquire" and "Once Divided," from *There Are Three.* Copyright 1998 by Donald Revell. Reprinted by permission of Wesleyan University Press. "Mechanics," from *My Mojave.* Copyright 2003 by Donald Revell. Reprinted by permission of Alice James Books.

Martha Ronk: "Reading Sappho," "Elgin Marbles," and "Still life: to name, to want," from *Desire in L.A.* Copyright 1990 by Martha Clare Ronk. Reprinted by permission of the University of Georgia Press. "Arroyo Seco," "Not Knowing the Language," "Neutra's Window," and "The Moon over LA," from *State of Mind.* Copyright 1995 by Martha Ronk. Reprinted by permission of Green Integer. "They say it might rain," "The folding screen," and "Ars poetica," from *Eyetrouble.* Copyright 1998 by Martha Ronk. Reprinted by permission of the University of Georgia Press. "[If I say I don't believe you is this impatience]," "[The paragraph she gives me to live in is I don't know how]," "Ophelia over the pond," and "Why knowing is / (& Matisse's *Woman with a Hat*)," from *Why/ Why Not.* Copyright 2003 by the Regents of the University of California. Reprinted by permission of the University of California Press. "A Photograph of a Plate Glass Window," "Some Birds," and "After Watching Jules et Jim," from *In a Landscape of Having to Repeat.* Copyright 2004 by Martha Ronk. Reprinted by permission of Omnidawn Publishing. " A failing memory" copyright 2007 by Martha Ronk. Reprinted by permission of the author.

Aaron Shurin: "All That," from *A's Dream.* Copyright 1989 by Aaron Shurin. Reprinted by permission of O Books. "A's Dream," "Saturated," "Sailed," and "Human Immune," from *The Paradise of Forms: Selected Poems.* Copyright 1999 by Aaron Shurin. Published by Talisman House. Reprinted by permission of the author. "Little Madrigal," from *A Door.* Copyright 2000 by Aaron Shurin. Published by Talisman House. Reprinted by permission of the author. "Involuntary Lyrics: XXIV" and "Involuntary Lyrics: LXXIII," from *Involuntary Lyrics.* Copyright 2005 by Aaron Shurin. Reprinted by permission of Omnidawn Publishing.

Carol Snow: "Prospect (*The Graces*)," "Positions of the Body VI," "[The Upward Is Endless]," "Frame," and "Bridge," from *Artist and Model.* Copyright 1990 by Carol Snow. Published by Atlantic Monthly Press. Reprinted by permission of the author. "Pool," from *For.* Copyright 2000 by the Regents of the University of California. Reprinted by permission of the University of California Press. "Bit," from *The Seventy Prepositions.* Copyright 2004 by the Regents of the University of California. Reprinted by permission of the University of California Press.

Susan Stewart: "Medusa Anthology," from *The Forest.* Copyright 1995 by the University of Chicago. Reprinted by permission of the University of Chicago Press. "The Seasons" and "Wrought from the generation of EARTH," from *Columbarium.* Copyright 2003 by the University of Chicago. Reprinted by permission of the University of Chicago Press.

Cole Swensen: "January" and "Sightings," from *Numen.* Copyright 1995 by Cole Swensen. Reprinted by permission of Burning Deck. "The Landscape Around Viarmes," from *Noon.* Copyright 1997 by Cole Swensen. Reprinted by permission of Green Integer. "The Invention of Streetlights," from *Goest*. Copyright 2004 by Cole Swensen. Reprinted by permission of Alice James Books. "The Hand as Historical" and "The Bones of the Wrist," from *The Book of a Hundred Hands*. Copyright 2005 by Cole Swensen. Reprinted by permission of the University of Iowa Press. "Windows in Paintings," "Versailles of the Scattered Here," and "Of the Insistent Equations of Opposites," copyright 2007 by Cole Swensen. Reprinted by permission of the author.

Rosmarie Waldrop: "Feverish Propositions," "Conversation 1: On the Horizontal," "Conversation 2: On the Vertical," "Conversation 3: On Vertigo," and "Conversation 4: On Place," from *Curves to the Apple*. Copyright 2006 by Rosmarie Waldrop. Reprinted by permission of New Directions Publishing Corporation. "The Grandeur of the Mountains," from *Love, Like Pronouns*. Copyright 2003 by Rosmarie Waldrop. Reprinted by permission of Omnidawn Publishing. "A Form of Lingering," and "The Body in the Word," from *Splitting Image*. Copyright 2005 by Rosmarie Waldrop. Published by Zasterle. Reprinted by permission of the author.

Marjorie Welish: "Respected, Feared, and Somehow Loved," "Veil," "Skin," "Moses und Aron," and "The World Map," from *The Annotated "Here" and Selected Poems*. Copyright 2000 by Marjorie Welish. Reprinted by permission of Coffee House Press. "[translation]" and "[translation]," copyright 2007 by Marjorie Welish. Reprinted by permission of the author.

Elizabeth Willis: "The Tree of Personal Effort," "Arthur in Egypt," "Three Apples, Two Chestnuts, Bowl, and Silver Goblet; or, The Silver Goblet," "Constable's Day Off," and "Drive," from *Turneresque*. Copyright 2003 by Elizabeth Willis. Reprinted by permission of Burning Deck. "On the Resemblance of Some Flowers to Insects," "The Great Egg of Night," "The Steam Engine," "A Description of the Poison Tree," "Her Mossy Couch," and "Ferns, Mosses, Flags," from *Meteoric Flowers*. Copyright 2006 by Elizabeth Willis. Reprinted by permission of Wesleyan University Press. "Why No New Planets are Ejected from the Sun" and "19 Short Films about John Wesley Hardin," copyright 2007 by Elizabeth Willis. Reprinted by permission of the author.

About the Editor

Reginald Shepherd is the editor of *The Iowa Anthology of New American Poetries* (University of Iowa Press, 2004). He is the widely anthologized author of five volumes of poetry, all published by the University of Pittsburgh Press: *Fata Morgana* (2007), *Otherhood* (2003), a finalist for the 2004 Lenore Marshall Poetry Prize, *Wrong* (1999), *Angel, Interrupted* (1996), and *Some Are Drowning* (1994), winner of the 1993 Associated Writing Programs' Award in Poetry. A 1993 "Discovery"/ *The Nation* Award winner, he has received grants from the NEA, the Illinois Arts Council, and the Florida Arts Council, among other awards and honors. Shepherd lives with his partner, the cultural anthropologist Robert Philen, in Pensacola, Florida, where magnolias and live oaks are evergreens.